AF342043

SPOTS FROM THE LEOPARD

O

Short stories of Aberdeen
and the North-east

By the same author—

Aberdeen.
Deeside.
Donside.
Buchan.
Kincardineshire.
Kalendar of Saints.
Let's Look Around Aberdeenshire.
Mediaeval Elgin.
Mediaeval Edinburgh.
North-eastern Journey.
A Buchan Tower-house.
City by the grey North Sea.
Royal Valley.
Legends of North-east Scotland.

The arms of the city and royal burgh of Aberdeen displayed on the cover of this book is from the copper stamp used for marking Aberdeen linen during the 17th century.

The leopard supporters first appeared as part of Aberdeen's armorial bearings in the year 1430. In heraldry, they typify warriors who have performed some bold enterprise with force, courage, promptitude and activity. It is possible the Aberdeen leopards refer to the prowess of the citizens in the cause of Robert the Bruce.

" 'Tis man's worst deed
To let the 'things that have been' run to waste,
And in the unmeaning present sink the past.''
—C. Lamb.

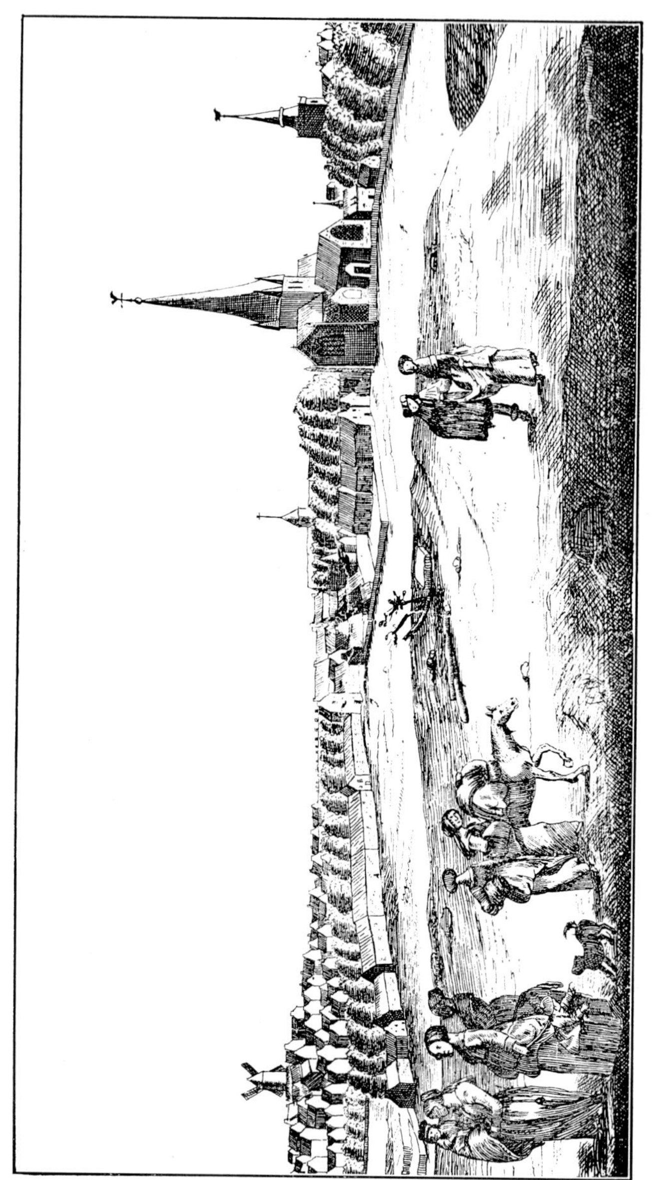

Aberdeen in the year 1661.

SPOTS FROM THE LEOPARD

●

*Short stories of Aberdeen
and the North-east*

FENTON WYNESS

IMPULSE BOOKS

ABERDEEN

First published 1971 by
IMPULSE PUBLICATIONS LTD.,
28 Guild Street,
Aberdeen, Scotland.

© Fenton Wyness, 1971.

Printed in Scotland by
ALEX. P. REID & SON,
28 Market Street, Aberdeen.

For

FRED,

companion on many forays

"In tim of valth, all men sims frendly,
An frind is not knawin bot in adversitie."

(Towie-Barclay motto: A.D. 1593).

CONTENTS

Page

NOTE: The small numerals in the text of the
book indicate the Appendix numbers.

ILLUSTRATIONS

FOREWORD

Spots from the Leopard is a collection of short stories dealing with a variety of subjects which have interested me over the years. Perhaps the word "interested" is an understatement—some of them have delighted, intrigued and occasionally mystified me. A number of the stories have already appeared in print and for permission to include them in this book I am indebted to the Editors of the following newspapers and magazines—*The Evening Express, The Press and Journal, The Scottish Annual and Book of the Braemar Gathering, Scotland's Magazine, The Scotsman* and *The Scottish Field. "The guidin' o't"* was commissioned by H.M. Ministry of Information during the Second World War for circulation in Russia.

It is with pleasure that I record my indebtedness to my friends W. J. Cramond, Esq., M.B.E., and Frederick G. P. Casely, Esq., F.S.A.Scot., for the generous help they have given me, and gratefully acknowledge the assistance given by Miss M. Wilkie, F.L.A., and Mrs. V. Robb of the Aberdeen Public Library Reference Department.

FENTON WYNESS.

45 Salisbury Terrace,
Aberdeen.   15th August, 1970.

ACKNOWLEDGEMENTS

The author and publisher desire to record their grateful thanks to the following for facilities granted in regard to the publication of photographs—

William S. Bell, Esq.

Frederick G. P. Casely, Esq., F.S.A.Scot.

Corporation of the City of Aberdeen—
Art Gallery Committee:
Public Library Committee:
Town Clerk's Department.

Edward Meldrum, Esq., A.R.I.B.A., F.S.A.Scot.

National Portrait Gallery of Scotland.

L. B. Perkins, Esq., B.Sc.

Society of Antiquaries of Scotland.

Society of Friends (Aberdeen Meeting).

George Washington Wilson (from the author's collection).

I

A PARSON'S BEDFELLOW

"Map me no maps."
—Fielding.

IT is strange how one sometimes forms a strong attachment to a piece of creative work yet knows little or nothing of the person whose perception and skill brought it into being. Many people have such attractions for old maps and, should they belong to Aberdeen, Gordon of Rothiemay's fascinating plan of the city will certainly be one of them. Dated 1661 and dedicated to the provost and magistrates of that time, Gordon's map—being the first "delineation" of the burgh—has been the basis for all subsequent plans of Aberdeen and on it every local historian since Gordon's time has built up his theories on the city's past.

Occasionally, reproductions of Gordon's map appear in sale-rooms and fetch fair prices for these are now regarded as "collectors' pieces". Few purchasers, however, know very much about the map-maker himself—an example of a remarkable achievement outliving the fame of the person whose abilities produced it—yet Gordon's own story is an extremely interesting one.

The old saying *"the Gordons hae the guidin' o't"* is true in a wide range of that family's activities. Cartography was no exception. James Gordon, the "delineator" of the Aberdeen map, was a worthy member of the illustrious House

1

of Gordon and his descent can be traced from the founder of the family. Of Norman extraction, the Gordons settled in Scotland during the early part of the 12th century. They first obtained a foothold in Berwickshire, but in the 14th century in recognition of their services to Robert the Bruce (1306-1329), received a grant of land in Strathbogie, Aberdeenshire. In 1376, Bruce's grant was confirmed in favour of Sir John Gordon of Strathbogie who died unmarried leaving two natural sons by Elizabeth Cruickshank of Aswanley in the parish of Glass—the famous "Jock" and "Tam". James Gordon the map-maker was descended from "Jock", the laird of Essie in Rhynie.

James Gordon was the 5th son of Robert Gordon of Straloch by his wife Katherine Irvine, daughter of Alexander Irvine of Lynturk. Born in 1615, James was one of a family of seventeen. Robert Gordon of Straloch was a noted cartographer and has to his credit the well-known map of contemporary Scotland for Bleau's *Atlas of the World* published in 1654. In this great work, Gordon was assisted by his son James who inherited much of his father's tastes and abilities, especially in map-making, and was artist as well as author.

James Gordon received his education in Aberdeen, graduating M.A. at King's College in 1636. At the age of twenty-six, he was appointed minister of the parish of Rothiemay in Banffshire, where he remained—Parson Gordon—until his death at the age of seventy-one.

In 1643, Parson Gordon, who incidentally was laird of Euchrie in the Banffshire parish of Marnoch, married Margaret Gordon, sister to James Gordon, laird of Rothiemay, by whom he had two daughters. Parson Gordon was a most conscientious minister as the parish record shows, yet he found time to pursue his other interests such as writing, drawing and map-making. As an author, Gordon's principal contribution is his *History of Scots Affairs from 1637-1641*, but it is as a map-maker that he is most widely known.

From about the year 1642 onwards, all Parson Gordon's spare time appears to have been occupied in preparing "planes and lyknesses" of the various Scottish burghs including Edinburgh, St. Andrews and Cupar. These maps have a quality all their own and possess that quaint, intimate touch aptly described by a well-known Scottish writer who says— "Given wings, one feels it would be possible to 'land' in their streets and walk in the shadows of the high-pitched houses, with many a pleasing glimpse of well-ordered gardens".

Gordon's map of *New and Old Aberdeen* is perhaps the most attractive of all his "lyknesses". The provost and magistrates of the burgh thought so too for on 16th October, 1661, the Council Minutes tell that the map which "Maister James Gordon, minister of Rothiemay, had bein att gryt paines in draughting upon ane meikle cairt of paper" was "weill done" and "in token of their thankfullness", the Dean of Guild is authorised to "buy or cause maik ane silver peece or cup wechant twentie vnces, and to buy ane silk hat and to dilyver to ye sayd Mister James with ane silk goon to his bedfellow".

Parson Gordon must have felt "gey braw" in his new silk hat but unfortunately his "bedfellow", Margaret Gordon of Rothiemay, did not live long to enjoy her silken "goon" for she died the following year. However, Parson Gordon married again, his second wife being Katherine Gordon. One can only hope that fashions did not change so frequently in the 17th century as they do today and that the second "bedfellow" derived some pleasure from Aberdeen Town Council's gift.

Parson James Gordon of Rothiemay died in 1686. He had many Aberdeen connections and it is interesting to recall that he was uncle to Robert Gordon (1668-1731), founder of the Hospital, now Robert Gordon's College.

2

THE CONSTABLE'S KEYS

"Two massy keys he bore of metals twain,
The golden opes, the iron shuts amain."

—John Milton.

IN the strong room of the Town House are kept the "official" keys of the City and Royal Burgh of Aberdeen. Beautifully made in silver, they are 18th century replicas of the original iron keys which were probably those of Aberdeen Castle and the Shiprow Port, the principal gateway into the town from the south.

Today, of course, the keys have purely a symbolic significance and rarely leave the Town House except on special occasions, such as an official visit from the Sovereign, to whom they are offered by the Lord Provost as a token of the City's loyalty to the Crown. This emblematic act of homage has its origin in early times when the custody of the Royal Burgh's keys was a serious matter—the function of a Crown official styled the Constable of Aberdeen.

Like many another Crown appointment in mediaeval times, the Constableship of Aberdeen was a hereditary office attached to the lands of Kermuck—originally *carn a' muick* (cairn of the pig)—near Ellon, just as the hereditary office of Mair of Fee—H.M. Collector of Taxes—was tied to the lands of Pitmuxton in Aberdeen (see Chapter 5). Like all such positions, the Constableship of Aberdeen was armigerous, the holder displaying on his own armorial bearings an inescutcheon charged with the keys of Aberdeen.

The office of Constable is first mentioned in the 13th century records when the appointment was held by a member of the Kennedy family of Kermuck. Originally, they came to north-east Scotland from Galloway where at an early date the family had settled from Ireland.

The lands of Kermuck lie to the north-east of Ellon and here the Kennedys had their stronghold—a motte-and-bailey structure of earthwork and timber. Nothing of the Kennedys' castle remains but it stood near the farm of Mains of Kinmuck —a modern spelling of Kermuck—and its site is marked on the Ordnance Survey Map of the district.

The Kennedys acquired other territories in the neighbour-hood of Ellon including Ardgith. This eventually became their principal possession and there they erected a stone-built tower-house, the ruins of which form a picturesque feature within the grounds of Ellon Castle.

In the early days, the Constables had their official quarters near the castle of Aberdeen, probably on the east side of the Castlegate where other Crown employees had their "lodgings". It would seem the Kennedys "over and beyond the line of duty", took a keen interest in the affairs of the burgh for in 1242, John Kennedy, the Constable, established a convent in the Shiprow. This was dedicated to St. Catherine of Sienna and finally gave its name to the hill on which it stood—St. Catherine's Hill, now covered by the buildings in Adelphi. The convent was ruled by the Grey Sisters of the Order of St. Catherine but how long they remained in Aberdeen is a matter of speculation. The convent's chapel, however, survived until the Reformation (1560) but was completely ruinous by the time that Parson James Gordon of Rothiemay made his map of the burgh in 1661. Today, a reminder of the Grey Sisters of Sienna is the name of St. Catherine's Wynd—the passageway which runs from Union Street to the Netherkirkgate. It is possible that the carved stones forming a picturesque archway in the boundary wall on the west side of the Shiprow may have come from the convent, while the stone baptismal font from the chapel is preserved in a local garden.

In the year 1652, a bitter dispute arose between John Kennedy of Kermuck, Constable of Aberdeen, and his neighbour Thomas Forbes of Waterton, near Ellon. The quarrel terminated in a hand-to-hand fight between Kennedy and Forbes when the latter was severely wounded and soon after died. Kennedy the Constable was accused of murder. He disappeared from the Ellon district but was subsequently captured and imprisoned in Edinburgh. From there he escaped and fled north to the lonely island of Stroma in the Pentland Firth where he remained in seclusion. His lands and property were forfeited to the Crown. Kermuck was then purchased by John Moir, 1st of Stoneywood, who in 1668 transferred it to Sir John Forbes of Waterton, son of the murdered man. Forbes immediately claimed the hereditary office of Constable, but the douce, determined citizens of Aberdeen refused to accept him so long as John Kennedy was alive. The Court of Session upheld their case. Yet, in 1669, when Sir John Forbes matriculated his arms at the Lyon Court, he claimed the right—as proprietor of Kermuck—to display the inescutcheon of Constable of Aberdeen. His claim was admitted by the Lord Lyon but it was not until John Kennedy's death on Stroma that Sir John Forbes of Waterton was confirmed in the office of Constable by Act of Parliament.

Three centuries have passed and the question is sometimes asked—has the office of Constable of Aberdeen ever been annulled? Probably not, and it would be interesting to know who today has the right to the hereditary office and to the honour of displaying the coveted inescutcheon—the crossed keys of the City of Aberdeen.

3

THE FREEDOM LANDS

"Lat the meithis and marches of the burgh
be weil keiped in all partis."
—Alexander Skene.

WHILE moving about the city, one is surprised to find in some unexpected place an object resembling a milestone, and astonishment naturally increases when the inscription is read—"ABD. 12"—or some other numeral. For example, at the lower end of Great Western Road—just over a mile from the city centre—two such stones are seen standing less than forty yards apart—"ABD. 3" and "ABD. 4"—little wonder that the amusing, though misleading name, *The Short Mile*, has been given to the neighbouring bar. They are not milestones, of course, but boundary stones or "march-stanes" as they are called in north-east Scotland.

Aberdeen is unique in possessing two distinct sets of these boundary stones marking what are known as the Inner and Outer Marches. Of the two sets, those of the Inner Marches are undoubtedly the older, but how much older is a matter of conjecture.

Today, town-planners glibly refer to "green-belts" encircling modern cities as if the idea was something new, whereas Aberdeen had its "green-belt" fully eight hundred years ago. In mediaeval times, Aberdeen was a small, compact burgh located on the estuary of the Denburn. Surrounding it lay a stretch of arable land—a "green-belt" set apart for the raising of crops and for the pasturage of cattle. Originally called the "burrow-roods", this stretch of land later became known as "The Crofts"—a name still met with in old feu charters. The designation of several of "The Crofts" gives some indication of their age, for example "Kennedy's Croft" and "Greathead's Croft", both these families having flourished in the burgh during the 13th century. The boundaries of "The Crofts" were the Inner Marches of the Royal burgh and were generally referred to as the "Regality". Thus the march stones of the Inner Marches have the letters "C. R." (City Regality) to distinguish them from those of the Outer Marches marked with the contraction "ABD." for Aberdeen. Where the boundaries of the Inner and the Outer Marches coincide, two stones are usually found side by side, one with "C. R." the other with "ABD.".

The Outer Marches are the boundaries of what are called the "Freedom Lands" of Aberdeen.

In the month of September, 1319, King Robert the Bruce visited Aberdeen where he was no stranger. He was given a tremendous welcome by the citizens, many of whom were his former comrades-in-arms. It is obvious from the city's records, that Bruce and his family had a strong affection for Aberdeen. They had first come to the burgh in 1306, weary, friendless and destitute, and had found shelter and loyal friends. By this time, King Robert's second daughter Matilda, was married to Thomas Isaacs, the Town Clerk, so the family's ties with the burgh had become more personal. Well pleased with the reception he was given in Aberdeen, and mindful of the help he had received in the past, King Robert granted a charter, gifting to the citizens in perpetual feu, his Royal "forest of Stocket"—a hunting forest lying to the west of the burgh. This charter, which was given at Berwick on 10th December, 1319, is one of Aberdeen's greatest treasures.

To the Stocket Forest, three other properties were subsequently added—Rubislaw, granted to the burgh by King Robert II in 1379; Cruives (Woodside), purchased by the magistrates from John Bannerman of Elsick and confirmed by James III in 1465; and Fittie, which over the years had been gradually absorbed into the burgh, and was formally approved by James VI in 1601. These collective properties formed the "Freedom Lands" of Aberdeen, and the revenues derived from it initiated the Common Good Fund, which today is valued at around half-a-million pounds sterling.

The acquisition of the Stocket Forest brought responsibilities and in 1398 arrangements were made by the magistrates for its protection and maintenance. Accordingly, foresters were appointed to guard the territory and it is interesting to note that the familiar name "Foresterhill" derives from this 14th century office. Such names as Forest Avenue and Road, Forest Gait, Mid Stocket Road, Stockethill Avenue and Crescent, are all reminders of Robert the Bruce's generous gift.

For over a century, the citizens of Aberdeen enjoyed the privileges of the Stocket Forest. However, in the year 1493, they were rudely shaken when it was announced that the late king—James III—had granted the Forest and the Castlehill of Aberdeen to Sir Andrew Wood of Largo, the celebrated Scottish Admiral, and that he intended sailing north to claim his gift. The citizens were stunned—but not for long. The provost, Alexander Reid of Pitfodels, hastily summoned the citizens to meet him on the Heading Hill and to a man they determined to fight for their rights. In due course, the gallant Admiral's flag-ship *The Yellow Caravel* was sighted off Girdleness but it would seem that Sir Andrew either sensed opposition, or had been informed of it, so he tactfully "retreated". Shortly after, the provost proceeded to Edinburgh carrying with him the proof of ownership—Bruce's charter of 1319—and on 20th June, 1494, letters under the Great Seal of King James IV were issued confirming the burgh's ownership of the Stocket Forest.

James III was an inveterate gambler, especially at cards. Sir Andrew Wood was his most regular opponent and it is on record that the king was frequently in his admiral's debt, sometimes for quite large sums. It is possible, therefore, that the king's gift of the Stocket Forest and the Castlehill may have been made in settlement of a gambling I.O.U. At all events, whatever the reason, the Royal aberration had the Aberdonians worried.

Following this unfortunate incident, the magistrates appear to have been more assiduous in the maintenance and protection of the "Freedom Lands". At first, the bounds had been fixed by natural objects such as hills, streams and boulders, but by the 16th century, "new maid saser stanes" were beginning to replace the original markers—a "saser" (saucer) being incised on the stone's surface. A few of these "saser stanes" survive but the significance of this particular mark has never been explained. Since then, other types of boundary stones have been set up to replace the older varieties, the present ones being marked "ABD" with the appropriate numeral. Originally, there were eight boundary stones on the Outer Marches, while today there are sixty-seven—including the "Alpha" (first) and "Omega" (last) stones which are common to both the Inner and Outer Marches.

The annual inspection of boundaries is of very ancient origin and has been known by various names—"Rogationing", "Beating the Bounds", "Ryding the Landymyres" and more recently "Riding the Marches". It was originally a religious ceremony performed during the Rogation Days—the three days before Ascension Day.

The ceremony is first mentioned in the City's records of 1398—the same year in which the Stocket Foresters were appointed—when several of the magistrates are designated *"Lineatores"*—linesmen or boundarymen. The first written description of a "Ryding of the Landymyres" is dated 5th May, 1525—on Holy Cross Day—during the provostship of Gilbert Menzies of Findon—the famous "Banison Gib" of local history. It is a brief but interesting description of the Outer Marches and mentions such well-known places as "Queylits" (Cults), "Bellies Wals" (Baillieswells), and "Stany Wode" (Stoneywood).

The Outer Marches were again "rydand" in 1531 and at intervals thereafter, the last Riding of the Marches taking place with great ceremony on 4th September, 1889. The provost at the time was Sir William Henderson—the first of our modern provosts to wear the civic robe which, incidentally, was purchased in 1877 so that Aberdeen's representative at Queen Victoria's Jubilee in Westminster Abbey might be suitably attired.

The year 1551 proved to be one of the most critical in the City's financial history for the burgh had run very short of money. Accordingly, in order to relieve their immediate embarrassment, the magistrates and certain of the burgesses formulated a scheme to feu the "Freedom Lands" for certain fixed feu duties plus an immediate money payment. Of course, their scheme required Royal assent before it could be put into effect, so the magistrates laid their proposals before Mary Queen of Scots who immediately acceded to their request—on the down payment of 2,500 merks, the Royal Exchequer being equally short of ready money. On 8th February, 1551, the magistrates availed themselves of her permission and feued the "Freedom Lands"—the majority of the feuars being none other than the magistrates and the burgesses themselves. Of course their action was bitterly resented by the citizens who saw their precious patrimony vanish before their eyes. Within a few years, the burgh had parted with the bulk of Robert the Bruce's gift—for the sum of £180 stg. and a fixed annual income of £70 stg. Had the magistrates of 1551 not made this financial blunder, the City of Aberdeen would now have been one of the wealthiest Corporations in the country. Perhaps the most striking example of what was lost in 1551 is the Estate of Hazlehead which was feued to Robert Chalmers for the sum of £13 : 6/8d. Scots (roughly £1 : 3/- stg.), and having passed through various well-known families, was subsequently purchased by the Corporation of Aberdeen in 1920 for £40,000 albeit for the benefit of the citizens whose heritage it actually already was. It says much for the succeeding controllers of our City's finances that "The Common Good" still flourishes, since the advantages lost in the 16th century have in some measure been retrieved.

Down the centuries, the ceremonial accompanying the Riding of the Marches has varied. For example, in 1531, they were ridden by only a few citizens appointed by the magistrates for the purpose, while in 1546 "the haill nicht-bouris of the toune" were ordered to attend the "Rydand" which took place on the Monday after Whitsunday. Disputes regarding the boundaries having arisen in the year 1580, a very solemn Riding of the Marches was ordained, and in 1594 the ceremony was combined with a great "Wappinshawin" (military parade) of all citizens of military age, when the "pomp and splendour of the Riding was such that it has never been surpassed".

In 1661, an important addition was made to the "Riding" when the magistrates appointed "Gilbert Gray, son of Thomas Gray, the provost" to be bearer of the burgh's Standard. Thereafter, the "lifting of the Standard" from the Town House became an important part of the ceremonial and the Standard-Bearer "mounted on his stately steed, caparisoned in ancient fashion" led off the procession from the Castlegate —at seven a.m.

An interesting report of the *"Ryding of the Landymyres"* was published in 1840—the joint production of Joseph Robertson, the historian, William Duncan and James Bruce. It makes fascinating reading today for it gives details of previous "Ridings" such as that of 1755 when the City Chamberlain had to foot the bill for the hire of "sixty horses at one shilling per horse—£3, plus 2/-d. for getting the horses ready". At that "Riding", carriages and gigs were much in evidence.

At Stone No. 31, on the farm of Wynford, west of Brimmond Hill, lies the "Doupin' Stane", a large flat granite boulder marking the westmost point on the Outer Marches. Here, an important part of the "Riding" ceremonial was enacted—"The Doupin' ", a procedure of ancient origin, going back to the days before estate plans when it was essential to secure a succession of living witnesses to the boundaries. "Doupin' " was believed to make a lasting impression on the mind, if not elsewhere, and the ceremony is quaintly described by Francis Douglas, the 18th century writer and Aberdeen printer:—"Two of the company, doup-free burgesses (burgesses who had already been "douped"), will take the novice by the shoulders, and two will lay hold of his legs, lifting him breast-high above the point of the rock, to which they will return his posteriors with a velocity proportionate to their respect for his character. The elevation and depression being thrice repeated, the person will be enrolled as a free brother-burgess''.

The last Riding of the Marches took place on Wednesday, 4th September, 1889. It was fully described by Robert Anderson in his book *The Riding of the Marches* and in a delightful *Sketch-book* by ''Dot''—the pseudonym of Robert Brough, A.R.S.A., the noted Aberdeen artist—for coverage by press photography was then unknown.

On this occasion, a dignified start was made from the Castlegate at nine a.m. This was followed by what was described as ''an injudicious gallop'' and on passing over Union Bridge the first casualty occurred—a Press reporter was unhorsed when his mount shied at a puff of smoke from a passing train. Thereafter, spills were fairly frequent, for the horses appear to have taken exception to the brass bands posted at various points along the route—as one reporter tactfully put it, ''much of the horsemanship displayed was open to criticism''. Eventually, the ''Doupin' Stane'' was reached and here the time-honoured ceremony took place. At Tulloch farm, in the quiet hollow between Brimmond Hill and Elrick Hill, the entire company sat down to a sumptuous Civic Luncheon—with many toasts. Thereafter, the ''Riding'' was resumed—but not by all, as the poet tells:—

> *"There were feastings and great drinkings*
> *On Brimmond's heathy side,*
> *And many a brave Town Councillor*
> *Unsteady homeward hied.*
> *Yes, many a civic member*
> *Of his limbs lost all control,*
> *And some were seen in armour bright*
> *Inviting lamp-posts on to fight,*
> *And did not go to bed that night.*
> *But home at morning stole."*

However, the procession eventually reached Aberdeen in the gathering dusk at six p.m.

4

R U A D R I ' S   T O U N

"The cross shines forth in mystic glow."
> —V. Fortunatus.

ONE of the oldest names associated with the city of Aberdeen is Ruthrieston. In the remote past, the lands of Ruthrieston were included in the extensive Celtic province of Mar whose Mormaers, or Chiefs, are on record from 1014. In that year, Donald, son of Emin, Mormaer of Mar, fell in battle at Clontarf helping the Irish under Brian Boru to repel an attack of the Danes. The last of these Mormaers was Ruadri who became first feudal Earl of Mar. He witnessed several Royal charters during the reigns of Alexander I (1107-1124) and David I (1124-1153) and is noted in the famous *Book of Deer*. From Ruadri, the ancient line descended to Thomas, 10th Earl of Mar, who died in 1377. He was the last of the male line of the Celtic Earls.

It is from Ruadri, last Mormaer and 1st Earl, that Ruthrieston derives its name—"Ruadri's toun", which lay within the area. It was a typical stronghold of the period consisting of a flat-topped conical mound of earth, surrounded by a ditch and crowned by a wooden palisade within which stood a timber-built tower. This type of stronghold is called a "motte". Early maps of Ruthrieston indicate the site— between the southern end of Ruthrieston Circle and Ruthrieston Road—but nothing now remains of this interesting link with Celtic times.

Ruadri's stronghold was strategically important. It dominated the most easterly ford over the River Dee which was then the main access to Aberdeen from the south, centuries before the building of the Bridge of Dee. It also dominated the road leading from the ford to the old Deeside road— now Broomhill Road—then the main route to the west. Here, at the north end of the ford where the roads branched, stood Ruadri's gallows which, curiously enough, long outlived his stronghold for the "gibbet at Ruddrystoun" survived until the 17th century. Its site was obliterated on the formation of Holburn Street. The only reminders of Ruadri the Mormaer is his name and the heraldic symbol used by his descendants the feudal Earls of Mar—the Crusaders' gold cross, the *"cross crosslet fitchee"*—seen today on the armorial bearings of Ruthrieston Secondary School and on other achievements linked with the district and with Mar. In the name "Dee Ford", the Church of Scotland's hostel in Riverside Road, is a reminder of the historic crossing on the Dee before the bridge was built.

In the earliest description of the area, Ruthrieston is called the "foul muir" and tells of its being a barren place where nothing grows but "furz, broom and hedder, there being many swamps, springs and streams". The accuracy of this description is proved by the street-names Auchinyell (Gaelic: "barren field"), Broomhill, Springbank, Thorngrove and Wellbrae.

Until the formation of Holburn Street and Great Western Road, only two main roads passed through Ruthrieston—the Hardgate and the old Deeside road. The Hardgate led from the centre of Aberdeen to the already-mentioned ford over the Dee near Ruadri's "toun" and subsequently to the Bridge of Dee, while the Deeside road branched off from the Hardgate at the north end of Fonthill Road and proceeded westwards to Braemar by what is now Broomhill Road and

Auchinyell Road. It is difficult to imagine that along this busy bus route, two once famous stage-coaches travelled—*"The Royal Highlander"* and *"The Earl of Aboyne"*.

Next to Ruadri's "toun", the most historic property in Ruthrieston was Pitmuxton. A pendicle of Ruthrieston, Pitmuxton is first mentioned in the year 1309 and was quite an extensive property. Its history is given in Chapter 5.

The building of the Bridge of Dee may be regarded as the first major development in Ruthrieston's history. It was the vision of Bishop William Elphinstone who died in 1514 without seeing his project carried out. However, the building of the bridge was undertaken by his successor Bishop Gavin Dunbar, who completed it in 1527. Skilfully widened in 1841, the bridge is one of the most impressive pieces of mediaeval architecture in the country. In 1693-94, to improve the access to the Bridge of Dee, the Aberdeen Town Council erected the Pack Brig over the Ruthrieston Burn. This bridge still stands although its original character was destroyed by the introduction of parapets when it was re-built in 1923.

With the building of the Bridge of Dee, came increased traffic and increased trade. On account of this, several small communities sprang up alongside the improved access to the burgh. These communities were known as cot-touns, groups of small, heather-thatched huts, the dwellings of people engaged in agriculture or fishing, or perhaps in the various trades such as weaving. Near Margaret Place stood the cot-toun of the lax (salmon) fishers, while near the Park Hotel in Riverside Drive stood the cot-toun of Ruthrieston associated with the neighbouring stance where monthly markets were held chiefly for the sale of cattle and horses. This market continued until comparatively recent times and to it the once popular "Museum Inn", still standing in Holburn Street, owes its origin. A monthly horse market was also held at Mannofield. Other cot-touns in the area included

Facing.   1. Arms of the Constables of Aberdeen.
            2. Key of the Shiprow Port.
            3. Bruce's Charter of 1319.

1   2

3

1

2

Pitmuxton and Tillyneedly, both obliterated by modern development.

After the Jacobite Rising of 1745, things began to move slowly in Ruthrieston. Parts of the "foul muir" were then enclosed and cultivation started by a few stout-hearted pioneers in agriculture. These "enclosures" as they were called, were the beginnings of the farms which, in our own time, have vanished from the scene—Newlands, Ruthrieston, Upper and Lower Kaimhill, Braeside and Garthdee. One of Ruthrieston's most progressive pioneers was Robert Balmanno whose story is told in Chapter 20.

By the beginning of the 19th century, a number of mansion-houses had been built in the area—Ashley, Forbesfield, Morningside and Broomhill, but of these only the first two survive. Thorngrove followed and is distinguished as being the first private house in the city to be lit by electricity.

When the Deeside Railway opened in 1853, Ruthrieston had the distinction of possessing two stations—Holburn Street and Ruthrieston. The district now began to develop rapidly for it was obviously a suburb with a future. Thus, blocks of land were acquired, developed and feued by various bodies such as the Incorporated Trades. The Hammermen are recalled in several of the street-names—Hammerfield Avenue, Hammersmith Road and St. John's Terrace, St. John the Evangelist being the Trade's patron. From 1900 onwards—except for the interludes created by two World Wars—Ruthrieston's development has been quite remarkable although the most spectacular changes have taken place during the past twenty-five years. It has come a long way from the days when it was simply the "foul muir".

It was not until the end of the 19th century that Ruthrieston became one of the Municipal Wards. Since its inclusion as such, Ruthrieston's boundaries have been altered several times, yet, despite these variations, the historic core of Ruadri's "toun" still lies within the Ward.

Facing. 1. Ruthrieston Pack bridge.
        2. Ruthrieston plaque.

C

5

MAIR OF FEE

*"But in this world nothing can be said
to be certain, except death and taxes."*
—Benjamin Franklin.

IN the year 1889, an Aberdonian, resident in Lausanne, Switzerland, asked a question in a then popular Scottish publication:—

> "In a garden on the east side of Salisbury Terrace, stands a house which looks very much as if it were a piece of neglected antiquity, and resembles a little the old house of Rubislaw now demolished. Can anybody tell me if it is really a piece of antiquity, or if it is built in a style to look old?"

His query was never answered and early in the present century the "piece of neglected antiquity" disappeared. No vestige of it remains, but a plaque marks the site and here is its story.

In 1306, during the First Scottish War of Independence, a weary, sick and dispirited sovereign made his way to Aberdeen where, with his consort and his family, he rested for several months. This was Robert the Bruce (1306-1329). In 1308 he again visited the Royal Burgh for which he had formed the deepest affection, as witnessed by his later benefactions to the town.

The following year King Robert gifted the lands of Pitmuxton to one of his friends, "Hugo of Aberdeen", the grant carrying with it the hereditary office of Mair of Fee—His Majesty's Collector of Taxes.[1]

Originally, the lands of Pitmuxton included all the territory south of Great Western Road to the River Dee. They were bounded on the north by the lands of Rubislaw, on the east by Ferryhill—roughly the line of Nellfield Place and Great Southern Road—and on the west by the lands of Ruthrieston—approximately the line of Gray Street.

From the Royal Burgh of Aberdeen, Pitmuxton was reached by the old Deeside highway—now Broomhill Road—which branched off from the Hardgate at its junction with Fonthill Road. In early maps of the district the "manour of Pitmuxton" is clearly shown with its cot-toun and mill. The mill was driven by the Pitmuxton Burn which had three branches—the first rising in Seafield Road, the second at the foot of Salisbury Terrace, and the third in Balmoral Road. The site of this once famous mill was on the north side of Allenvale Road—on what is now the newer part of Allenvale Cemetery—while on the south side stood, or rather stands—for a later house now occupies the site—the "Outseats of Pitmuxton", now contracted to "Outseats".

"Hugo of Aberdeen" was succeeded in Pitmuxton—and of course as Mair of Fee—by a member of the celebrated Keith family, but early in the 15th century Pitmuxton passed to Robert Blinseil who in 1482 was elected provost of Aberdeen. Soon after his election to the civic chair, Blinseil granted to the Altar of the Blessed Virgin Mary in the Kirk of St. Nicholas an annual rent of two merks from the lands of Pitmuxton for the celebration of an obit for himself and his wife Isabella Wood on the anniversaries of their deaths, and for the purchase of thirteen loaves and a "quantitie of goode fleche" for distribution among thirteen poor persons.

The next occasion on which Pitmuxton is mentioned in the burgh's records is in 1647, when an outbreak of the plague, or "the pestilence" as it was then called, spread terror and death throughout Aberdeen. Despite the rigid military guard placed at all crossings over the River Dee and the stringent regulations taken for the "weill and saiftie of the toun", the plague was carried into Aberdeen by a woman from Brechin.

She settled in the cot-toun of Pitmuxton and died there three days later, having in that short time infected several unfortunate people. Thereafter, the plague spread rapidly and in the next few months more than 1,760 people out of a population of 8,000, succumbed.

Twenty years after the "visitatione" of "the pestilence", the lands of Pitmuxton were acquired by Andrew Skene, 2nd of Ruthrieston, and his son Andrew given "the office of mair of fee in the Sheriffdom of Aberdeen". Andrew Skene, 3rd of Ruthrieston, succeeded to Pitmuxton in 1668. He was a prosperous "paynter and glassenwright" whose grandfather Robert Skene, 1st of Ruthrieston, acquired the property in 1615. For over a century, the Skenes retained possession of Pitmuxton, but on the death of Dr. David Skene, 5th of Pitmuxton, in 1770, the property passed to George Allan.

It was probably during the ownership of the Allans—sometime between 1893 and 1899—that the name Pitmuxton disappeared and Pitstruan was substituted, the former meaning "place of the pigs" and the latter "place of the small burn"—probably the Salisbury Terrace burn already referred to. The name Allan Street commemorates the Allan family's connection with Pitmuxton.

The historic "manour house" of Pitmuxton stood on a site immediately south of the Salisbury Place entrance to the Ruthrieston Sports Ground. A plaque now marks the site. The house faced south-east and its tree-lined avenue led from the old Deeside highway—now Broomhill Road—where the Broomhill Garage now stands.

Pitmuxton House and its "laich-biggins" were extant in 1899 and until recent years the house-well could be seen in the back garden of No. 39 Salisbury Terrace. It seems likely that the old house of Pitmuxton was built by the Skenes *circa* 1670, in all probability on, or near, the site of an earlier construction, and its resemblance to Rubislaw House may have been more than coincidence for the latter was built in 1675 by another branch of the Skene family.

The early years of the present century saw the general disintegration of Pitmuxton House. Ere that time, its fine policies and gardens were being utilised as market gardens and by the outbreak of the First World War, nothing of the old house remained. With the opening of Ruthrieston Sports Ground, the last traces of the historic property vanished and to the hundreds who make use of the facilities there, the name ''Pitmuxton'' conveys nothing.

6

OUR LADYE OF GOOD SUCCESS

"So easie a thing it is for fables to find good harbour."
—Father Gilbert Blakhal.

THE story of the miraculous statue of *Our Ladye of Good Success* appears to be founded partly on fact and partly on fiction. It is therefore difficult, after the lapse of over four centuries, to separate reality from romance. The statue of *Our Ladye* is in itself no figment of the imagination for it is one of the most treasured possessions of the parish church of Finistere in Brussels.

The statue is said to have been part of the plenishings of the Cathedral of St. Machar, Old Aberdeen, where it adorned the Chapel of Our Lady during the rule of Bishop Gavin Dunbar (1518-1532). Tradition tells that the bishop spent long hours in prayer before it and that the Blessed Virgin audibly directed him where to build the projected bridge over the River Dee at Ruthrieston. That this story was then circulating in Aberdeen is substantiated by Alexander Kennedy, a Franciscan monk in the monastery of St. Augustine, Brussels, who, in a declaration made on oath and dated 19th May, 1636, avers he had the facts from his Aberdeen ancestors. The suggestion, frequently expressed, that the statue of *Our Ladye of Good Success* at one time adorned the west front of St. Machar's Cathedral may be discounted while the statement that it was over six hundred years old in Bishop Dunbar's time is without foundation. The design and craftsmanship of the statue which is of wood and probably of Flemish origin, completely rule out these assertions.

From recorded evidence, we learn that the building of the Bridge of Dee—the dream of Bishop William Elphinstone (1483-1514)—was commenced about the year 1520 by Bishop Gavin Dunbar and was completed in 1527. Its site, whether or not dictated to the saintly bishop by supernatural means, was the only possible one—west of the existing ford and conveniently placed for access from the Causey Mounth route. As was customary at the time, a wayside chapel for the devotions of those setting out on, or returning from a journey, was included in the building scheme. It was a small, simple structure, situated at the north-east end of the bridge and dedicated to Mary, the Blessed Virgin. It was to this chapel at the Bridge of Dee that Bishop Gavin Dunbar—according to tradition—gifted the statue of *Our Ladye of Good Success*, having received in its place a finer figure of St. Mary wrought in silver for the chapel in the Cathedral of St. Machar.

On 14th December, 1529—after protracted negotiations— the responsibility for the upkeep of the Bridge of Dee and its chapel was accepted by the magistrates of Aberdeen. The following year—on January 9th—appears the name of the chapel's first incumbent, Sir William Ray "umquhyle chaplane to our ladye chappell of the Bridge of Dee". It would appear that Ray had but recently vacated the chaplaincy and had "deliverit in judgement to the bailzeis and counsaill" the following items from the chapel—"ane silver crucifix, ane chaleis of silver, ane ymage of Our Ladye of silver baicht ouir guilt (variegated with gold), thre naipkingis ane broodin (embroidered) and twa quhyt, ane altar towell, togedder with the key of the offerand stok (offertory box), to be kepit to the utilitie and profitte of the said chappell". From the description given in the above inventory, the "ymage of Our Ladye" would seem to be identical with *Our Ladye of Good Success*.

The reason for Sir William Ray demitting office is not mentioned. It has been suggested that he was the only priest to hold office in the Bridge of Dee chapel and that his resignation in 1530 was due to the approaching change in religious belief and that the chapel was already falling into disuse—after only three years! These suggestions can hardly be accepted, for the magistrates, acting on instructions from the Church, were at this time taking strong measures against the precepts of Martin Luther in an endeavour to keep the burgh "clene of all sic filth". The Reformation was still thirty years away.

A month after Sir William Ray had relinquished his duties —in February, 1530—a dispute arose over access to the River Dee between the chapel and the bridge. It would appear that a parapet impeded the passage of fishing gear belonging to James Gordon of Abergeldie, and in the tradition of the time, the feudal baron immediately caused the obstruction to be "dinged doon". However, Provost Gilbert Menzies took the matter to the Committee of Estates in Edinburgh, but as the subject does not appear again in the Council's Minutes, the outcome is unknown—although the laird of Abergeldie made good the damage.

The Reformation came to Aberdeen on 4th December, 1559, when a wild and lawless rabble swept into Aberdeen from the south. The "dool and destruction" wrought by them on the monasteries and churches in the burgh is well known, but oddly enough, information regarding the chapel at the Bridge of Dee is completely lacking. Father Gilbert Blakhal in his *Breiffe Narration*, written in 1666-67, recounts the story of *Our Ladye of Good Success* and tells "that this statu was thrown in the sea at Aberdein". This is actually the first record we have of the legend—if fable it is—for what is more likely than that "Knox's rabble" would pillage the first religious building in their path on crossing the Bridge of Dee, seize the effigy of *Our Ladye*, and cast this symbol of the hated Faith into the river? The swift-flowing waters would carry it down stream the short distance to the estuary

—then the harbour, for the course of the Dee was diverted in 1869. Here, lying at anchor, would be ships from many lands and the floating figure—"silver, baicht ouir guilt"— would surely attract the attention of some mariner who would naturally retrieve it if only as an unusual piece of flotsam or, should he be of the ancient Faith, rescue it with loving care and give it a place of honour on his ship.

At all events, tradition tells that the figure was picked up in Aberdeen harbour by a merchant captain from the continent who conveyed it to Ostend, reaching port on the day when a battle between Spanish Catholics and Netherland Protestants was at a critical stage. It is said the arrival of the ship with the statue of *Our Ladye* on board turned the tide of battle in favour of the Spaniards and victory followed.

During this period, the Low Countries were under Spanish rule, the Regent being the widowed Duchess of Parma—the Infanta Margaret of Spain, aunt of Philip II. The Infanta held office for ten years and was Regent when the statue of *Our Ladye* arrived at Ostend in 1560. Naturally, she heard of the victory and of the statue. Father Gilbert Blakhal continues the story in his *Breiffe Narration*—the Infanta "did send for the statu to be brought to Brussels, wher the princesse, with solemne procession, did receave it at the porte of the tune, and place it in this chappelle, wher it is much honoured, and the chappelle dedicated to *Our Ladye* of bonne successe, which befor wes pouer and desolat, now is riche and wel frequentit".

The Infanta placed the statue in the safe-keeping of the monks of St. Augustine's Monastery in Brussels where it remained until transferred by command of Napoleon I to the parish church of Finistere in the same city.

In the year 1860, when the Cathedral of St. Mary of the Assumption in Huntly Street, Aberdeen, was dedicated, the Very Reverend John Sutherland endeavoured to have the statue of *Our Ladye of Good Success* returned to Aberdeen. He sent a plea to Pope Pius IX (1846-1878). However, the Holy Father replied that, while he would be pleased to see

the statue of *Our Ladye* returned to Aberdeen, he had no
jurisdiction in Brussels over Church property, consequently
could not ordain its return. The Churchmen of Brussels
would not part with it, so *Our Ladye of Good Success* remains
there, venerated on her feast day—the Assumption of Mary
the Blessed Virgin—on 15th August.

A very fine replica of the statue of *Our Ladye of Good
Success*—originally called *Our Ladye of Bon-Accord*—adorns
St. Peter's Roman Catholic Church in Justice Street, Aberdeen.

7

"UNCLEAN! UNCLEAN!"

"Allone, with-outen any compayne."
—Chaucer.

WHEN the typhoid fever epidemic of 1964 was at its height in Aberdeen, the city was likened to a leper colony—an exaggeration, of course, but it did bring home to many people the devastating effects of ostracism, if only for a few weeks. Yet in bygone times, sufferers from this dread disease had to face banishment for life.

Like most Scottish burghs, Aberdeen had its leper colony and until recent times the ground set aside for sufferers from this disease was called "Lepers' Croft", a name still found in old charters and title deeds. It comprises that area of land now bounded on the east by King Street; on the south by Nelson Street; on the west by Mounthooly and King's Crescent; and on the north by what was formerly Advocates' Road. "Lepers' Croft" lay almost equidistant between Aberdeen and Old Aberdeen on the main route north. Three hundred years ago, the croft was the most dreaded part of the neighbourhood for here the lepers lived—or existed—in complete isolation in what was called "The Lazar House", St. Lazarus being the lepers' patron.

In those days, of course, no attempt was made to cure the afflicted sufferers, the main idea being to keep them from contaminating the healthy. Thus the regulations drawn up for lepers were both harsh and rigid. For example, on no account must a leper drink or wash at wells or streams used by healthy people; the "unclene" must drink and wash within their "Croft" at the "Lepers' Myre", a very unsavoury marsh —enough to make the most diligent Medical Officer of Health blanch. Any breach of rules meant certain death by hanging. As the Gallows Hill was conveniently situated to "Lepers' Croft", it was an ever present reminder of the penalty to be paid for infringement.

The lepers were granted 4d. per day which they could augment by begging for alms along the roads they travelled. When food was scarce, the lepers were compelled to beg within the burghs "to ye perell of clene folkes" and to herald their approach, were obliged to carry a hand-rattle or bell and call out "Unclean! Unclean!" as they moved about. By an Act of James VI (1567-1625), the lepers were given the right to take one peat from every load exposed for sale in the market-place, the Aberdeen lepers having a further claim to one peat from every load passing along the highway bounding their "Croft". Lepers were strictly forbidden to leave their "Croft" after sundown.

Today, it is difficult to realise that the busy site off King Street, now partly occupied as a bus depot by the Aberdeen Corporation Transport Department, should have been a leper colony. Yet a chapel was built in 1519 by Alexander Galloway, the philanthropic parson of Kinkell, near Inverurie, on the ground now occupied by Nelson Street Roman Catholic School. Dedicated to St. Anna, the chapel was for the use of lepers living on the "Croft" who, of necessity, were denied entry into places of worship although a few churches did make provision for them. Records tell that the site for the chapel was given by the Provost and Magistrates of Aberdeen to the "puir ladies", presumably a sisterhood of St. Lazarus devoted to work among the lepers.

It would seem that by the year 1574, leprosy was beginning to die out in north-east Scotland for the "Lepers' Croft and Myre" were duly sold. However, the canny magistrates of

Aberdeen retained the "Lazar House"—"just in case"—and earmarked the proceeds from the sale for "uphalding the said house and sustenation of the lipper-folkis that sal be thairin". It would appear that the last sufferer to occupy the "Lazar House" was "ane puir woman infectit with Leprosie" to whom the key was delivered in 1604. She must have died shortly after for by the year 1661 Parson Gordon of Rothiemay records—"such as goe out at the Gallowgate Port towards Old Aberdeen, half way almost, may see the place where of old stood the lepers' hospital, called the Seick Hous". The ruins of "Seick Hous"—the "Lazar House"—were still visible when G. and W. Paterson made their plan of Aberdeen in 1746. Thereon styled the "Sickhouse Ruins", they disappeared before the end of the century.

However, unknown to a great many people, there still remains in Aberdeen an interesting tangible reminder of the lepers. On the north wall of the ruined kirk of St. Fittick in Torry, there is to be seen a small, rectangular window, now bricked-up. The infilling is unfortunate for it completely obliterates the window's unique character, it being one of the very few examples of its kind in Scotland. The window is what is known as a "lepers' squint"—an opening set obliquely through the kirk wall so that those suffering from the disease might see the altar and follow the service from outside the building without being seen by, or coming in contact with, the congregation. It is a unique link with a sombre chapter in the City's history when the pitiful cry "Unclean! Unclean!" struck terror into the hearts of the inhabitants.[2]

8

THE   BLACK   ARTS

" 'Tis now the very witching time of night."
—Shakespeare.

ABOUT forty years ago, a workman engaged in some repair work to a very old property in Aberdeen made an astonishing discovery. Below the granite hearth-stone of the fireplace in the principal room, he found the complete skeleton of a cat. The workman was naturally very curious about his "find" for the hearth-stone weighed fully a ton and had every appearance of having been in position since the house was built some four hundred years ago. How did the outstretched skeleton get there?

The explanation is almost as fantastic as the workman's "find" for he had accidentally stumbled upon an unusual link with the past—that remarkable period in the city's history when witchcraft was at its height. The cat-below-the-hearth was an extremely interesting example of a house-holder's endeavour to secure protection against witchcraft or the "working of woe" as it was then called. He had securely "laid" a witch's "familiar"—in this instance a domestic cat.

Although witchcraft is as old as time, it was not until the end of the 16th century that its practice reached the point when Church and State were obliged to take drastic action to stamp out the "evils of sorcerie and witchcraft". In Aberdeen, the first victim of this purge was Barbara Card "ane notorious vitch", who in 1590 was condemned to death by burning. Some four years later, a few unfortunate old women were put to death in a similar manner but the real "witch-hunt" of the century began in 1596. It followed a Commission issued by King James VI (1567-1625) for the "Haulding of Justice Courtis on Witches and Sorceraris", and it lasted a full year.

The "witch-hunt" of 1596-97 is surely the most ghastly chapter in the city's history, and the records carefully preserved in the city's strong-room are of unique interest today for they are the actual documents used during the Trials of the unfortunate wretches accused of "Sorcerie". The Commission of King James empowered ministers and elders of the Church of Scotland to examine all persons suspected of witchcraft and to submit in writing a "dittay" or accusation against such persons. Of course, the Commission afforded vindictive people ample scope against their enemies and in reading over some of the charges made against the accused, one wonders how any minister of the Gospel could possibly testify as many of them did. There is obviously a strong element of personal animosity in several of the "dittays" and many of the accusations are quite fantastic.

For example, the causing of influenza appears to have been a favourite charge and several of the witches were accused of "working woe" in this way. In the quaint wording of the "dittays", the unfortunate victims of witchcraft suffered great pain "the one half of the daye being rossin as in ane ovin, the other half melting away in ane extraordinare caul sweat". Of course all the witches were accused of attending "Dueilische meetings" when the "De'il" himself appeared to receive their homage.

The locus of these "Dueilische meetings" is interesting— the Fish Cross in the Castlegate, the Gallows Hill near Trinity Cemetery, Pocra Quay and other centres around the city. However, the most popular rendezvous of the Aberdeen witches was St. Catherine's Hill, now covered by the buildings in Adelphi. It would appear that the largest "Conventione" of witches and warlocks ever held in Aberdeen took place here on 25th September, 1594—doubtless within the ruined precincts of St. Catherine's Chapel. At the early hour of "thrie of the morning" and by way of Andrew Gow's Close in the Shiprow, the witches and warlocks forgathered on St. Catherine's Hill, then a grass-covered mound with some fine old trees. Here, the "sorceris dansit a lang space some rydand on trees" and it is recorded that the "De'il" himself provided the dance-music played "on his owin forme of instrumentis".

During the appalling "witch-hunt" of 1596-97, twenty-four people, mostly elderly women, were brought to Trial, found guilty and condemned to death by burning. It would seem that these witch-burnings became quite a public attraction for at the execution of Margaret Clerk "foure sparris biggit to withstand the press of the pepill" were broken by the spectators and had to be replaced by the Town Council at the heavy cost of 8/8d.

The scene of these witch-burnings was the grassy hollow lying between Castlehill and the Heading Hill—the hollow now called Commerce Street. The accounts for the burnings are still preserved and tell their own gruesome story—"peattis, coillis, tar, fir, ane staike and ane faddome of tow". For his trouble in dispatching the unhappy victims, the public hangman received a gratuity of 13/4d. while the Dean of Guild—being of professional status—and who had "extraordinarlie taken paynis on the borning of the gryt number of witches" received the handsome honorarium of £47 3s. 4d. Scots. from the grateful Town Council.

A contemporary writer tells that "for days on end the awful black reek and stink from the burnings laye heavy ower the Castlegate"—but it passed, and with it the most sinister twelve months in the burgh's history.

Facing.   1. Our Ladye of Good Success.

2. Old St. Fittick's, Torry.

1

2

1

2

3

9

THE WALLACE TOWER

THE fascinating building popularly known as the Wallace Tower, stood in one of Aberdeen's oldest and most historic streets, the Netherkirkgate—the nether, or lower road leading from the Castlegate to the "toun's kirk of St. Nicholas". It was for long the sole survivor of the original buildings lining the Netherkirkgate and its picturesque character never failed to attract the attention of visitors to the city. Like some doughty old warrior who had braved many battles, it was held in the deepest affection by the citizens who regretted its demolition in 1964.

The site in the Netherkirkgate on which the Wallace Tower stood is, in itself, of considerable historic interest. From the middle of the 12th century, the land belonged to the Knights Templars and on the suppression of the Templars in 1312, their "temple-land", as it was called, passed into the hands of that other Order of Chivalry the Knights Hospitallers— the Knights of the Hospital of St. John of Jerusalem. The Netherkirkgate "temple-land" remained in the Hospitallers' possession until the Reformation (1560) when Sir James Sandilands, the last prior of the Order in Scotland, resigned all the Hospital properties to the Crown. In 1563, however, Mary Queen of Scots erected these properties into a temporal

Facing.   1. Fertility Charm.
          2. James VI and I.
          3. The Wallace Tower, Netherkirkgate.

D

barony in favour of Sir James Sandilands and his heirs, Sir James assuming the title of Lord Torphichen—after the Hospitallers' chief possession in West Lothian.

The Netherkirkgate "temple-land" thus became part of the barony of Torphichen and so it remained until 1588 when Lord Torphichen disposed of it, along with other lands, to Thomas Hamilton, later Lord Binning. In the same year, Hamilton sold the "temple-land" to Sir Robert Keith of Benholm in the county of Kincardine, and here Sir Robert erected the building subsequently known as the Wallace Tower.

Born in 1536, Sir Robert Keith of Benholm was the third son of William Keith, Master of Marischal, eldest son of William, 4th Earl Marischal. The Master of Marischal died in 1580, the year before his father, consequently the title passed to George, eldest brother of Sir Robert Keith of Benholm. George Keith thus became 5th Earl Marischal and was the founder of Marischal College, Aberdeen. In 1594, Sir Robert Keith obtained the barony of Benholm from his uncle Robert Keith, Commendator of the Abbey of Deer in Buchan, who had acquired it by marriage with Elizabeth Lundie, heiress of Benholm. Sir Robert was knighted in 1612.

Sir Robert Keith of Benholm would appear to have commenced building immediately on gaining possession of the Netherkirkgate site for his "lodging" was typical of the period—a Z-planned, fortified tower-house, similar in design to a number of other castellated buildings in Aberdeenshire such as Terpersie (1561), Pitcaple (*circa* 1570), and Cluny (1588). Benholm's "lodging" would seem to have been built between the years 1588 to 1590.

In the 16th century, the "lodging" occupied a strong strategic position for it stood at the head of Carnegie's Brae leading to the Green and the south, just outside the Netherkirkgate Port which it dominated. Even as late as 1800— before the formation of Union Street—the view from the "lodging's" south-west tower was described as being very extensive. Built at the time when firearms were replacing

the earlier means of defence, the "lodging" was well-equipped
with gun-loops for horizontal, flanking fire.   It was therefore
not by chance that Benholm's "lodging" was built on the
Netherkirkgate site.

The first owner of the house would appear to have been
as picturesque as the building.   Sir Robert Keith of Benholm
was a great trial to his brother George, the Earl Marischal,
and to his uncle the Commendator of Deer, and in 1590 the
tension among them reached breaking point.   Sir Robert,
with a band of accomplices, seized and garrisoned the Abbey
of Deer but was eventually dislodged by the Earl Marischal's
forces and escaped to Fedderate Castle where a truce was
eventually arranged.   Keith of Benholm died in 1616 and
shortly thereafter his Netherkirkgate house was purchased by
one of Aberdeen's most noted citizens—Patrick Dun, M.D.,
first lay Principal of Marischal College.

Patrick Dun was born in 1580.   He was the elder son of
Andrew Dun, burgess of Aberdeen, by his wife Mary Johnston,
and grandson of Charles Dun, litster, whose wife Christian
Mitchell was one of those unfortunate women burnt at the
stake for witchcraft in 1597.   Patrick Dun studied medicine
in Germany where he established a considerable reputation.
In 1619 he was appointed Rector of Marischal College and
two years later became its principal.

From his father, Patrick Dun inherited a considerable
fortune.   He acquired the lands of Tarty in the parish of
Logie-Buchan in Aberdeenshire which remained in the family
until the Jacobite Rising of 1745.   Patrick Dun is best remembered in Aberdeen for his munificence to the Grammar School
for by his will, dated 1633, he bequeathed to the school the
lands of Ferryhill, an exceptionally valuable gift which, had
it been properly administered by the Aberdeen magistrates of
the time, would have made the Grammar School not only
independent today but possibly the wealthiest school in Scotland.   Patrick Dun died in 1644 when Benholm's "lodging"
passed to his nephew Dr. Robert Dun of Tarty who, in turn
was succeeded by his son Patrick.   With this Patrick, the
the Duns' interest in the "lodging" ended.

Benholm's "lodging" next became the manse of John Menzies, Professor of Divinity at Marischal College. Born in 1624 John Menzies was the son of Gilbert Menzies, burgess of Aberdeen. He married Margaret, eldest daughter of Sir William Forbes, 1st Baronet of Craigievar, by whom he had a son—who predeceased his father—and three daughters, Margaret, Ann and Barbara. Brought up as a Roman Catholic, Menzies apostatised and in 1649 was appointed to the second charge of St. Nicholas Kirk. The following year, he transferred to Greyfriars and in 1679 was appointed to the Chair of Divinity at Marischal College. The author of several important works, John Menzies died in 1684. He was survived by his daughters—Margaret, the eldest, married to her kinsman Thomas Forbes, advocate, who owned the "lodging" for a time, and Barbara, the youngest daughter, who married William Hay of Balbithan who also possessed the "lodging" for a short period. Hay disposed of the property in 1669 to Andrew Logie.

Andrew Logie of Loanheid of Bonnietoun in the Aberdeenshire parish of Rayne, was the son of George Logie and grandson of the Rev. Andrew Logie, the anti-covenanting minister at Rayne. An advocate by profession, Andrew Logie married Anna, daughter of Alexander Paton of Kinaldie by his wife Isabel Keith. Logie had two sons—William and George—and a daughter Mary who survived her brothers and eventually became his heiress. Thus in 1709, Benholm's "lodging" passed to Mary Logie who in 1715 married William Wemyss, an Inverness merchant. William Wemyss subsequently purchased the lands of Craighall in the Aberdeenshire parish of Kennethmont, and for a time was the owner of the Netherkirkgate house. It is interesting to note that the first complete description of the Netherkirkgate site "lying without the Netherkirkgate Port of Aberdeen" dates from the Logies' ownership when the name "Benholm's Neuk" is used.

In 1755, the "lodging" was purchased from William Wemyss by James Abernethy, merchant, who retained possession until 1786 when it was acquired by James Niven. From this date run the feu charters of the property.

John Niven, a prosperous tobacco and snuff manufacturer was the son of James Niven, an Aberdeen merchant and perfervid Jacobite who was executed at Carlisle for participation in the Rising of 1745. The Nivens were a well-known Aberdeenshire family and owned the small property of Thornton, near Keith-Hall, Inverurie, which gave its name to Thornton Court in the Guestrow where the Nivens had their town house before moving to Benholm's "lodging". About the year 1770, John Niven added a wing to the old tower-house. This extended to the south—down Carnegie's Brae—and housed his kiln and other items necessary for his business. On the first floor of this wing, with access from the tower-house, was a finely proportioned room panelled in Scots pine, which doubtless served as Niven's business room and where he entertained his customers. Eventually, the Nivens removed from Aberdeen to Peebles and in 1789 the "lodging" was sold. From this date, nothing is heard of the family except that Niven's son Henry was subsequently knighted by King George IV.

In 1789, James Coutts, flax-dresser, became the owner of Benholm's "lodging". By this time, of course, the Netherkirkgate Port had been demolished and the name "Wallace Tower" applied to the "lodging" for the first time. Coutts continued in possession until 1851 when it was acquired by Donald Taylor, and he and his heirs remained until 1895. In that year, the "Wallace Tower" was purchased by James Pirie, spirit dealer, when the basement and ground floor were converted into licensed premises. In 1918, the property was acquired by the Corporation of Aberdeen and some thirty years later—with the introduction of the *Town and Country (Scotland) Act, 1947*—the "Wallace Tower", on account of its unique architectural and historical value, was listed under Category "B" viz.:—*"that its destruction would only be considered if necessary in the public interest"*.

However, in 1964 and despite strong public protest, Benholm's historic tower-house was demolished and today its site is marked by a plaque built into the north wall of the cat-walk, the *ersatz* Kirkgate of our time.[3]

10

AN ARTIST AND HIS FAMILY

"I desire you would use all your skill to
paint my picture truly like me, and not
flatter me at all."

—Oliver Cromwell.

IN an unmarked grave within the capital city of Scotland, rest the mortal remains of the country's first portrait painter, George Jamesone. In Edinburgh, where he lived and worked for some years, his only memorial are his paintings in the two National Galleries. Perhaps this is as it should be for, in the long run, an artist's memorial must surely be his work.

It is sometimes said of certain people that they are fortunate in their choice of parents and George Jamesone was clearly one of these. His parents were unusually gifted and much of their individual skill appears to have been inherited by their son. He was the third generation of artist-craftsmen and he, in turn, passed on something of his genius to three succeeding generations. Thus the Jamesone family's contribution to the arts in Scotland—and it covered a period of two hundred years—must surely be unique.

George Jamesone was born in Aberdeen in the year 1588— the exciting year of the Spanish Armada. He was the second son of Andrew Jamesone, "maister measone", and his wife Marjorie Anderson, both of Aberdeen. Andrew Jamesone was a son of William Jamesone, burgess of Aberdeen and "Dekyne" of the local masonic "Luge".

"Dekyne" Jamesone was a man of substance for he held the office of "maister measone to ye kirk and brig wark" of the burgh, a post corresponding to that of City Architect or Burgh Surveyor. Thus, when "Dekyne" Jamesone's son Andrew married Marjorie Anderson in 1585, he was a young man of means while his wife—a daughter of Gilbert Anderson, a prosperous merchant, and his wife Janet Moir—was equally well endowed. Marjorie's three brothers rose to positions of eminence—Alexander became Professor of Mathematics in the University of Paris; David, laird of Finzeauch, was the celebrated "Davy-do-a'-thing"; while John was a well-known "pynter" in Edinburgh. George Jamesone was therefore fortunate in his parentage for yet another reason—they provided him with a cultured home and with sufficient means for study and for the pursuit of any career he might care to follow. By some curious chance, George Jamesone selected an artistic career—portrait painting—then almost an unknown profession in Scotland.

Unfortunately, the house in which George Jamesone was born and lived for so many years is no longer in existence for, like so many historic properties in Aberdeen, it was swept away in the cause of "progress". Its demolition in May, 1886, after considerable public protest, was a two-fold tragedy, firstly as it was an exceptionally fine example of Scottish domestic architecture and an authentic example of Andrew Jamesone's work and secondly, as it was the birthplace and home of Scotland's first portrait painter. In any other town, of course, the house would certainly have been preserved for posterity and it is interesting to recall that one of the most ardent fighters for its preservation was Jamesone's fellow-townsman and a fellow-artist—Sir George Reid, President of the Royal Scottish Academy, whose beautiful drawing of the house is well-known. The house appears to have been built *circa* 1586 and was completed the year before George Jamesone's birth.

In 1598, George Jamesone was sent to Aberdeen Grammar School, then situated in Schoolhill a short distance west from the Jamesone's house. He remained there until 1601 when he entered Marischal College.

George Jamesone's art training appears to have commenced in 1612. In that year he was "prentized" for "aucht yearis" to his uncle John Anderson, "pyntour in Edinburgh", who would seem to have been born in Aberdeen *circa* 1586 and received his education in the burgh. He subsequently moved to Edinburgh where he established himself as an artist. Thus Jamesone's first steps in art were ably guided by a competent teacher. In 1616, however, Anderson returned to Aberdeen while Jamesone went to Antwerp to continue his studies.

There were, of course, a number of reasons why Jamesone should select Antwerp as a place to further his art training. Aberdeen and Antwerp had close commercial ties while the latter was the headquarters of the Painters' Guild of St. Luke which included Rubens and several of the great masters such as Jan Breugel.

Tradition asserts that George Jamesone entered the studio of the famous Rubens where he had Anthony Van Dyck as a fellow pupil. Confirmation of these assertions is lacking but they have caused Jamesone to be styled "the Scottish Van Dyck". This is regrettable, for apart from the obvious Flemish influence in the work of both artists, no comparison can be made between them. Much of George Jamesone's sojourn in Antwerp remains a matter of speculation but it is to be hoped that one day, the full story may come to light.

George Jamesone returned to Aberdeen in 1620 to receive his first important commission, a portrait of Sir Paul Menzies, provost of the burgh. So, by his own undoubted ability and with such influential patronage, Jamesone found his next few years fully occupied. In 1624, he married Isobel Tosche and settled down in his father's house in Schoolhill where he built a studio. Thereafter, commissions came in steadily and soon Jamesone's reputation as a portrait painter spread throughout Scotland.

In 1633, Jamesone visited Edinburgh for the Coronation of Charles I (1625-1649) when he was honoured by the king giving him sittings for a full-length portrait. It would seem the portrait was an unqualified success and Jamesone's name was made. He opened a studio in the capital where he worked for several years moving between Edinburgh and Aberdeen when commissions necessitated his being in the north.

It is no exaggeration to say that Jamesone painted nearly everyone of importance in Scotland at this time. His output was considerable as the lists of his paintings show, and although his fees were moderate he became a wealthy man. Jamesone acquired the lands and castle of Esslemont, near Ellon in Aberdeenshire, and in 1635 gave Aberdeen its first public park—"ane four-neukit gairden"—enclosing the then highly esteemed Spa Well which he restored and "embellished with his awin hand".

Yet despite his fame and his fortune, George Jamesone's life was not without its sadness. Never a robust man himself, his four sons predeceased him, consequently the direct line of artist-craftsmen came to an end when he died in Edinburgh in 1644. He was buried in Greyfriars' Kirkyard, but the actual site of his grave is unknown.

George Jamesone's three daughters, Isobella, Marjorie and Mary, were his heirs. Of Isobella little is known; Marjorie married an Edinburgh lawyer John Alexander and this union produced a line of famous artists; and Mary, an artist in her own right, married firstly George Aedie, magistrate of Aberdeen, and secondly her cousin James Gregory of the famous academic family. Mary Jamesone was the creator of the four unique needlework panels now preserved in the West Church of St. Nicholas, Aberdeen, the finest examples of their kind to be seen in Scotland today. Mary Jamesone inherited her father's self-portrait which remained in the possession of her descendants until 1923 when it was acquired by the Aberdeen Art Gallery.

A plaque now marks the site of George Jamesone's house in Schoolhill. He was a truly remarkable man whose family hold a pre-eminent place in the annals of Scottish art.

II

MURDER IN THE GREEN

"Murder most foul, as in the best it is;
But this most foul, strange, and unnatural."
—Shakespeare.

ALTHOUGH the murder of Brother Francis is briefly referred to in a number of Scottish histories, this horrible incident is not generally known. Obviously, the event has been glossed over, for the cold-blooded slaughter of this saintly man is one of the blackest chapters in the chronicles of Aberdeen.

The story begins in the year 1181 when William the Lion (1165-1214) built himself a "palace" in the Green, the then civic centre of the burgh. Only the merest fragment of this building—discovered by accident below the present street level —remains, but it is sufficient to prove the "palace" was a structure of some architectural merit.

About the year 1200, King William invited Pope Innocent III to send to Scotland some members of the Order of the Holy Trinity, a religious body founded in 1198 for the purpose of redeeming Christian captives from the infidels. The Pope accepted this invitation and accordingly a small band of Trinitarians, or Red Friars as they were generally called, came to Scotland. As sponsor of the Order, William the Lion made various grants of land to the Trinitarians and to show his personal interest in the Red Friars, gifted to them his "palace", garden and grounds in the Green at Aberdeen, thus introducing them to the burgh.

For over three hundred years the Friars remained in the Green where they worked and prospered. During these years, of course, they added various buildings essential to their growing establishment, the most important being the chapel which, in part, survived until 1794. Like that of most monastic institutions, the Friars' garden was an important feature and some of the fruit trees planted and tended by the monks long out-lived them. The ground covered by this productive garden was that busy area now bounded by Guild Street, Rennie's Wynd, Trinity Street and Stirling Street, and it is difficult to believe that as recently as 1731 the Friars' orchard was still bearing fruit. In that year, the "growing timber and big ash tree in the flower garden" was sold by public roup. Some of the fruit trees survived until the beginning of the 19th century.

In these pleasant and tranquil surroundings overlooking the estuary of the Den Burn, the Trinity Friars lived happily. However, no Golden Age ever lasts long and the Reformation broke upon them suddenly and with relentless fury. On 4th December, 1559, a wild and lawless rabble of Reformers swept into Aberdeen from the south exciting the citizens to fever pitch. Entering the burgh by the Hardgate and Windmill Brae, they crossed the Den Burn into the Green where they converged on the Trinity Friars' monastery.

In those far-off days, no police force could be called upon to protect life and property and so, from the start, "Knox's rabble" had it all their own way. First, the boundary walls were breached, priceless windows smashed, doors forced and several of the buildings set on fire. Then looting started. The church plate of gold and silver, the embroidered vestments and hangings, the carved and decorated images—all were valuable plunder to those who got in first. Nothing was sacred.

At this point in the uproar, one of the friars, Brother Francis, tried to reason with the mob. It would seem that the monastery's strong-room was situated on the upper floor of a tower reached by a narrow spiral staircase. Here, on the staircase, Brother Francis made a bid to save the treasures of his Order but in the turmoil was brutally struck down and stabbed to death. In an attempt to conceal their horrible crime, the looters cast his body into one of the burning buildings.

A few relics of King William's "palace" and of the Trinity Friars' Monastery may still be seen in Aberdeen but nothing remains to remind posterity of Brother Francis. Yet in an ancient church in the city of Palma on the island of Majorca, there is preserved a portrait of Brother Francis—the work of an unknown Spanish artist. Said to have been inspired by the famous Father Figueras, the "Champion of the Trinity Friars in Scotland", the portrait bears the inscription—

"Saint Francis of Aberdeen.

Martyred, 4th December, 1559."

12

WAS SHAKESPEARE HERE?

"All the world's a stage,
And all the men and women merely players."
—Shakespeare.

FOR many years, historians have debated the question whether William Shakespeare, the celebrated dramatist, visited Aberdeen. No documentary evidence has yet come to light to prove the point either way, but as so much of the playwright's own life—even his date of birth—is without documentation, one can only seek proof by circumstantial evidence.

From the city's records, it is clear that Aberdeen has long been "theatre minded", indeed it can claim to be the first Royal burgh in Scotland to present a stage production. This was in the year 1440 when local players produced "Haliblude" (Holy-blood), the story of the Last Supper. Of course this play had the backing of both Church and magistrates and although details are scant, it is noted in the records that the producer was granted £3 6/8d. Scots to cover staging expenses. "Haliblude" was an open air presentation, the locus of the entertainment being the Windmill Hill on the east side of the Gallowgate, opposite the Technical College.

Following the production of "Haliblude", "playes" became a regular feature and the burgh records show the popularity of these entertainments. They appear to have been mostly in the form of pageants and tableaux, the ''plot'' being a religious one. In the archives at Trinity Hall—the headquarters of the Aberdeen Incorporated Trades—there are many references to the miracle plays and pageants in which the trades took part, indeed during the 15th and 16th centuries, most of the ''supers'' for these performances were drawn from the trades.

About the year 1531, a new type of ''playe'' made its appearance in Aberdeen and became extremely popular. This dealt with the life-stories of the Saints, particularly with those of the martyrs whose blood-curdling deaths afforded great scope for the actors' abilities and taxed the ingenuity of the ''props'' men. Favourite subjects were St. Sebastian, his bleeding body pierced by numerous arrows; St. George destroying a fire-breathing dragon; the decapitation of St. John the Baptist; and of course St. Nicholas, patron of Aberdeen, with the three infants he restored to life following their recovery from a pickle-vat. It would seem that public taste for horrific entertainment has changed very little in the past four hundred years.

An enthusiastic patron of ''the playe'' was James VI (1567-1625) and when he visited Aberdeen, he was always much impressed by the productions presented in his honour by local actors. Thus in 1601, King James returned the compliment by giving the burgh its first taste of professional drama. In October of that year ''be reasoun they are recommended by His Maisties speciall lettir'', an English company from the Globe Theatre, London, visited Aberdeen for a three week ''season''. During that time, they were fêted by the magistrates and accorded a civic luncheon while their manager-producer, Laurence Fletcher, was made a Freeman of the burgh. The open-mindedness of the magistrates in permitting this English company to perform their ''playes and comedies'' in the burgh is to be commended for the same company met with very stiff opposition from the reformed clergy of Edinburgh. Unfortunately there is no record of the ''playes'' produced during this historic visit, but it is established that the production took place in "The Playe Field", near the Spa Well in Woolmanhill.

Apart from the name of Laurence Fletcher, no record has yet been found confirming the identity of the other players. Nevertheless, it has been suggested—and with good reason— that the actors who visited Aberdeen in 1601 were the same company which, in 1603, were granted a Royal Licence namely—Fletcher, Shakespeare, Burbage, Hemings, Condel, Phillips, Sly, Armin and Cowley.

Shakespeare began writing *Macbeth* four years after the Aberdeen visit, completing it the following year. This adds weight to the suggestion that the idea for the drama was given to Shakespeare when he visited the north-east in 1601 as Macbeth had in fact been killed at Lumphanan some twenty-five miles west from Aberdeen. Shakespeare is said to have taken the *Macbeth* story from Holinshed's *Chronicle* (1577), yet the introduction of the weird sisters and the scene on the "blasted heath" may well be accounted for by the fact that he himself crossed the dreaded "Mounth"—the Grampian Mountains—and was appalled by this desolate stretch of countryside. One day, perhaps, the missing links in the story of the dramatist's visit to the north-east will be found.

13

GRUESOME RELIC

*"Wild animals never kill for sport.   Man is the only
one to whom the torture and death of his fellow
creatures is amusing in itself."*

—Froude.

AFTER three hundred years, the reason why James Graham, 5th Earl and 1st Marquis of Montrose, changed sides during "the Troubles" of the 17th century, is still a controversial point among historians.   Born in the year 1612, he died an ignominious death at the early age of thirty-eight.   Tradition asserts that, at his birth, his mother the Lady Margaret Ruthven, second daughter of William, 1st Earl of Gowrie, consulted a witch whose prediction regarding the infant's future was subsequently given to the public by the boy's father, the 4th Earl of Montrose— "Jamie was to be a sair trial to Scotland".

Montrose's astonishing career is a matter of history and need not be detailed.   Enough to say that his last and probably his bloodiest battle was fought at Corbiesdale in Ross-shire, on 27th April, 1650—a well-planned ambush which cost Montrose dearly—400 killed and 600 taken prisoner out of a force of 1,200

Although severely wounded and with his horse shot from under him, the Marquis was miraculously dragged to safety

Facing.   1. George Jamesone's House, Schoolhill.

2. Brother Francis.

1

2

1

2

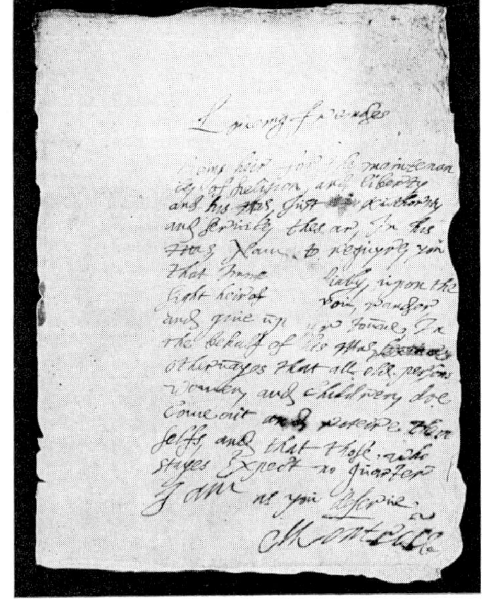

3

from the press of battle, remounted, and successful in escaping from the stricken field. He swam the Kyle of Sutherland and disguised as a shepherd made his way up Strath Oikell into the wilds of Assynt. Three days later, completely exhausted from his wounds, from exposure and starvation, Montrose reached Ardvreck Castle and threw himself on the good-will of a former comrade-in-arms, young Neil McLeod of Assynt. In doing so, the Marquis made his fatal mistake. With traditional Highland hospitality, McLeod welcomed his guest—then sold him to his enemies for 400 bolls of meal.

Montrose's long and tedious journey from Ardvreck to Edinburgh has frequently been described and the story told how, while in detention at Pitcaple Castle in Aberdeenshire, he was offered—but declined—the somewhat unsavoury means of escape by a *garderobe* flue.[4] At all events, on Saturday, 18th May, he reached the capital and the following Monday was brought before Parliament, tried for treason, found guilty, and sentenced to death.

Seldom has the viciousness of the Godly been more manifest in Scotland than it was in the instance of the death sentence passed on the Marquis of Montrose. For treason, the sentence for a nobleman was decapitation, but on this occasion, the vindictiveness and blood-lust of the Covenanters demanded much more—a public hanging as a common felon, followed by the butchering of his body, the principal burghs of Scotland each to receive a relic of their barbarity. His head was to be displayed on the west gable of Edinburgh's tolbooth; Perth and Stirling were each to receive an arm; while the legs were assigned to Glasgow and Aberdeen. The mutilated trunk was to be interred on the Burgh-muir alongside the vilest criminals of the time—a truly shocking display of Christian charity.

Facing.   1. The Well of Spa, Woolmanhill.
          2. Mummified arm of Montrose.
          3. Montrose's letter of 1644.

E

Montrose received his sentence calmly and with dignity. However, his innermost thoughts were succinctly expressed in the poem he wrote that night in the condemned cell:—

> *"Let them bestow on ev'ry Airth a Limb;*
> *Open all my Veins, that I may swim*
> *To Thee my Saviour, in that Crimson Lake;*
> *Then place my pur-boil'd Head upon a Stake;*
> *Scatter my Ashes, throw them in the Air;*
> *Lord (since Thou know'st where all these Atoms are)*
> *I'm hopeful, once Thou'll recollect my Dust,*
> *And confident Thou'll raise me with the Just."*

As it proved, the words were prophetic.

The melancholy story of the final scene in the crowded Market Place on Tuesday, 21st May, 1650, has often been recounted—the grim, black-draped scaffold with its thirty-foot gibbet; the various instruments of butchery conveniently arranged alongside the five deal boxes placed in readiness to receive their ghastly contents.

The execution took place at three o'clock in the afternoon. Three hours later, the dead Montrose was cut down and falling on his face was conveniently positioned for dismemberment with the axe. The mangled trunk was carried to the Burgh-muir—now called "The Meadows"—for burial while the limbs were packed for transport to their predetermined destinations. This was thought by the Covenanters to mark the end of an unpleasant chapter, but even in death "Jamie was to be a sair trial to Scotland".

The night of the execution, the freshly-dug grave on the Burgh-muir was rifled. Montrose's heart was taken from the trunk and carried back to Edinburgh where it was embalmed by James Calender, a skilled chirurgeon and apothecary. This was done on instructions from the Lady Elizabeth Erskine of Mar, wife of Sir Archibald, 2nd Lord Napier— the son of Montrose's sister, the Lady Margaret Graham—to whom Montrose had always promised his heart. An egg-shaped casket fashioned of steel from one of Montrose's own swords, was made to encase the heart and this was eventually enclosed in a gold filigree box—a gift from the Doge of Venice to John Napier of Merchiston, the inventor of logarithms. It would seem that the heart remained in Lady Napier's possession until her death when its peregrinations with various other members of the Napier family began. On the way to India, it was nearly lost in a naval engagement off the Cape de Verde Islands when the gold filigree box was shattered beyond repair. However, an Indian goldsmith produced a replica and also made a silver urn to contain the box. Montrose's heart remained in the Middle East for some years but in 1792 was returned to Europe. It was in Boulogne when the French Revolution broke out and a Scotswoman living there undertook to conceal the relic until it could safely be returned to Scotland. However, she died suddenly shortly afterwards and although a thorough search was made, Montrose's heart was never found.

The opening of Montrose's grave on the Burgh-muir and the removal of his heart, caused consternation among the Covenanters and fearing further activity, they had the grave deepened and protected. They also caused an iron cross-piece to be fixed on the Tolbooth's "trinket prick"—piercing the ears—lest an attempt be made to remove Montrose's head.

Of Montrose's dismembered limbs allocated to the four principal burghs, little is known except in the case of Aberdeen which, as before mentioned, had been assigned a leg. It would seem, however, that in the confusion following the removal of Montrose's heart, the boxes containing the severed limbs were wrongly consigned, for Aberdeen's gruesome reminder of the Marquis proved to be an arm—subsequently impaled on the spikes of the Justice Port and seen by King Charles II when he visited the burgh on Thursday, 7th July, 1650. By the king's command, it was removed and placed in Huntly's aisle of Our Ladye's Pitie Vault in the Kirk of St. Nicholas.

Eleven years passed. The first Parliament of the Restoration in Scotland met in Edinburgh on 1st January, 1661, and three days later sat again when it resolved "an honourable reparation for that horrid and monstrous barbarity fixed on Royal authority in the person of the great Marquis of Montrose, His Majesty's Captain General and Lord High

Commissioner; namely that his body, head and other his divided and scattered members, may be gathered together and interred with all honour imaginable''.

Accordingly, on 7th January, ''the trunk was collected from the Burgh-muir, wrapped in the finest linen and so incoffined'' while the head—or what remained of it after years of exposure to the elements and the avid attentions of the birds—was removed from the Tolbooth and added to the remains which lay in the Chapel of Holyrood-house until 11th May, 1661, the date appointed for the State Funeral.

In the interval, efforts were made by James, 2nd Marquis of Montrose, to assemble his father's scattered limbs but what reply he received from Glasgow, Perth and Stirling is obscure. From Aberdeen, however, the response was satisfactory and in the Minutes of the Town Council for 25th May, 1661, the following appears—''The said day, the counsell haveing informatione from Doctor James Lesley, doctor of medicine, that it was signified to him from Edinburgh by Captaine George Melvill, that it was the desyr of ane noble and potent Earle James Marques of Montrose, that the dismemberit part of the bodie of the late murtherit Marques of Montrose, his father, suld be socht out of the place of the church of this burghe wher the samen was interrit efter it was takin doune from the pinacle wher it was put up by the enimies of the said Marques, and that the samen suld be takin up and preservit till order suld come for transporting the samen to the bodie''.

The magistrates of Aberdeen immediately gave orders that Montrose's arm should be removed from Huntly's aisle ''coverit with ane reid crimpsone velvet cloth'' and carried in Civic State from the kirk of St. Nicholas to the Town House. Montrose's kinsman, Harry Graham, son of Sir Robert Graham of Morphie, had the honour of bearing the relic which remained in the burgh's ''high counsell hous till such tyme as order suld be sent for transporting thereoff''.

The State Funeral took place according to plan on 11th May, 1661, from Holyrood-house to the Cathedral of St. Giles where his remains were laid to rest ''at the back of the tomb of his grandfather'', John Graham, 3rd Earl of Montrose.[5]

What the coffin contained was never divulged. As regards the dismembered portions, the records of Glasgow, Perth and Stirling are silent, while no mention is made in the Minutes of the Aberdeen Town Council of the ''dismemberit part of the bodie'' having been forwarded to Edinburgh although this may have been done. Both Harry Graham and his father, the laird of Morphie, took part in the State Funeral.

Centuries passed, then in 1896 a paper was read to the Society of Antiquaries in Edinburgh by J. W. Morkill of Austhorpe, Yorkshire, who exhibited a dried and mummified right arm reputed to be that of James Graham, 1st Marquis of Montrose. The opportunity was taken to make careful examination of the relic and Sir William Turner, the noted Edinburgh anatomist, reported that it might well be Montrose's right arm. There was evidence of impaling on the palm of the hand and on the forearm as well as a deep wrist wound such as Montrose had received at the battle of Corbiesdale. J. W. Morkill had acquired the arm by purchase in 1891. The story of the arm—together with a note on Montrose's broadsword—was subsequently printed in *Proceedings of the Society of Antiquaries of Scotland* (14 : 12 : 1896), wherein are traced details of its ownership from 1712 onwards. The authenticity of these details is beyond question—but before that date there is only speculation.

As above mentioned, the arm sent to Aberdeen was exhibited on the Justice Port for just five weeks before its removal to Huntly's Aisle in St. Nicholas Church. There, it was carefully preserved until taken to the ''high counsell hous'' on 25th February, 1661. Thereafter, its history is unknown. Of the four dismembered limbs, the Aberdeen fragment is the only one whose record is known—up to the date mentioned, and it would seem to have been the best preserved. Is it possible, then, that the arm never reached Edinburgh for the State Funeral but was surreptitiously carried off to England as a prized relic of the great Montrose?

14

JACOBITE INTERLUDE

*"The old order changeth, yielding place to new,
And God fulfils himself in many ways,
Lest one good custom should corrupt the world."*
                                        —Tennyson.

MUCH of Aberdeen's history centres round the Castle-gate for it has been the hub of the city for upwards of six hundred years. Naturally, its character has changed with the passing of time yet today there are several reminders of its romantic past.

As mentioned in a previous chapter, it is to the erudite Parson Gordon of Rothiemay that the city owes its first "guide book"—his description and map of New and Old Aberdeen—and from this unique work we learn a great deal about the Castlegate. Prominent on Gordon's map, made just over a century after the Reformation, are what he describes as the "ruines of the Templairs neare the Justice Port". He tells that "upon the north syd of the Castlegate ther is to be seen amongst the gardings a certain obscure and scarcelie now decernible ruine or foundatione". This "ruine" was all that remained of the religious house possessed by the Knights Templars and later by the Knights Hospitallers, the site of which is now marked by a bronze plaque built into the ancient boundary wall—the "muckle dyke capped with eavedropes"—forming part of the western limit of the Market Stance, off Justice Street.

The well-known pend in Justice Street with its dignified entry designed by the architect John Smith, leads to St. Peter's Roman Catholic Church and Rectory. These buildings now occupy the ground formerly owned by the Knights Templars

—a truly remarkable example of "site-fixation"—for the Templars, champions of the ancient Faith, held the site from a very early period until 1312 when they were succeeded by the Knights Hospitallers whose ownership terminated with the Reformation in 1560. Thereafter, the land was divided into lots and sold to various purchasers. Thus it remained until the middle of the 18th century when, as a reunited "land", the Templars' property in the Castlegate was acquired by the Roman Catholic Church.

The exact date when the Knights Templars settled in the Castlegate is uncertain for their deed of foundation is lost—it was said to have been among the documents carried off to England in 1296 when Edward I visited the "cytie d'Abberden and taryed ther V dayes". Whether Edward of England stayed at the "faire castell" of Aberdeen or with the Templars is not recorded but it is possible he visited their establishment. The nature and extent of the buildings erected by the Knights Templars is a matter of conjecture but they certainly included a Hospice.

As already mentioned, the Templars' properties passed in 1312 to the Knights Hospitallers who had possession until the Reformation. Eventually, the Castlegate lands were acquired by Thomas, Lord Binning, from whom they passed to various owners.

By the middle of the 17th century, the buildings on the Castlegate site had become derelict—as Parson Gordon quaintly puts it "the very ruines are almost ruinated". However, the site was much too valuable to remain vacant for very long and by 1696 a number of "tenements" had been erected there. One of these, still standing, was the property of Alexander Scott, a prosperous shipmaster, who down the years acquired most of the other "tenements and lands". According to the custom of the time, the pend leading from Justice Street to Scott's properties took his name—Skipper Scott's Close—and as such became famous in Scottish history.

Skipper Alexander Scott was a perfervid Jacobite. On 2nd September, 1715, the Jacobite Standard was raised at Braemar and the following month George Keith, 10th Earl

Marischal, rode into Aberdeen to proclaim James Francis Stuart, the Chevalier de St. George, King James VIII and III. The Earl and his friends were duly wined and dined by the Incorporated Trades and for the next six months Aberdeen was in Jacobite hands. Skipper Scott took an active part in the Jacobite intrigues and he was a valuable asset to the cause—he owned a good ship, well armed, and was in regular contact with France.

The 23rd day of December, 1715, was dark and drear. A thick haar lay over Aberdeen's Castlegate masking the entry to Skipper Scott's Close. In the afternoon, a small party of horsemen wearing the uniform of French Naval Officers, rode into the close and dismounted. Here they were welcomed by Skipper Scott who "bent the knee" to one of his visitors—none other than the Chevalier de St. George—King James VIII and III. Unfortunately, the Chevalier was ill with influenza but after a hot meal and a dram under the hospitable Skipper's roof, he was able to ride on with his companions into the mist—and shortly thereafter into exile again.

In 1762, Skipper Scott's house and other "tenements" in the Castlegate were acquired by the Roman Catholic Church and eventually became the residence of the Vicars Apostolic and principal centre of the Faith in north-east Scotland. Here, Bishop James Grant, titular Bishop of Eritrea died in 1778 and Bishop John Geddes, titular Bishop of Morocco in 1799. For ten years—from 1862—the house was the headquarters of Mother St. Basil, foundress of the Congregation of the Poor Sisters of Nazareth, who with six others, came north to Aberdeen and established the first foundation outside Hammersmith, London—a home for the aged and orphan children—Nazareth House in Claremont Street.

The foundation stone of the present St. Peter's Church was laid in 1803 by the much-loved Priest Charles Gordon (1771-1855) and on the completion of the building the following year, High Mass was celebrated for the first time in Aberdeen since the Reformation. The wheel had made full turn in the story of the "Templairs neare the Justice Port".

15

S T A N E   H O O S E

"He builded better than he knew:-
The conscious stone to beauty grew."

—Emerson.

BUILT into the back wall of a property on the west side of Belmont Street, is one of the finest pieces of heraldic stone-carving to be found in the City of Aberdeen. In design, craftsmanship and historic interest, the panel is of unusual value.

The story begins in the year 1408 when the name Gilbert Menzies appears in a note of Aberdeen rentals, Gilbert's being the impressive sum of twelve pennies Scots. Four years later, he is mentioned as being a baillie of the burgh and in 1433 Gilbert was elected provost.

Gilbert Menzies was the younger son of Sir Robert Menzies of Weem in Perthshire who, with his brother William, came north to Aberdeen to make their way as merchants—and they most certainly did. Gilbert Menzies was the first of the name to occupy the civic chair and thereafter, the collective ''provostships'' of the Menzies family totalled a hundred and thirty years.

In 1454, Gilbert's eldest son Andrew was elected provost of Aberdeen. He is the first Menzies to be styled ''of Pitfodels'' which the family held for over four centuries. By this time, the Menzies had acquired an extensive piece of land lying on the south side of the Castlegate opposite the

Tolbooth. On this land, they subsequently erected a house—not a stone-built house as one might expect in such an important street, but a timber house complete with gallery and fore-stairs and "weil theikit with hedder" as was the custom at that date. The site of "The Laird of Pettfoddels House" is indicated on James Gordon of Rothiemay's map of 1661. It is now occupied by the Bank of Scotland. An extensive garden ran down to what is now Regent Quay. This "timmer hoose" of the Menzies passed from father to son and in 1525 it was owned by Gilbert Menzies, provost of Aberdeen. He occupied the civic chair for six terms covering a period of twenty-five years (see Chapter 18).

In January, 1527, the Castlegate house came in the news through a most unfortunate affair. Provost Menzies was entertaining some friends to dinner, among them two Aberdeenshire lairds, Alexander Seton of Meldrum, and John, Master of Forbes. The provost was a most hospitable man and the party dined well. However, after the meal, an argument arose between Forbes and Seton—the former being a hot-headed, quick-tempered man who could not brook contradiction. It would seem that, in the argument, Seton would not give way so the irascible Master of Forbes decided to settle the quarrel once and for all—he drew his sword and ran the unfortunate laird of Meldrum through.

About two years after the above incident, the Castlegate house caught fire and being entirely constructed of wood, was totally destroyed. In those far-off days before fire insurance, such disastrous fires might well have brought total ruin to the owners. However, the Menzieses were men of substance and so there arose on the Castlegate site a new house—a magnificent stone-built mansion, the like of which had never before been seen in the burgh. Completed about the year 1535, it was the first stone-built house in Aberdeen and it survived until 1766.

Unfortunately, no pictorial record of the house exists and the only fragment of the building to survive is the heraldic panel in Belmont Street. This bears the initials "T.M."—

Thomas Menzies of Pitfodels, who was provost of Aberdeen in 1525. The eldest son and heir of the already-mentioned Provost Gilbert, Thomas succeeded to his father's properties in 1543. He was wealthy, forceful and capable and in consequence had his enemies in the burgh council chamber who were not slow to tell him they ''were not feart, no, for all his power or his stane hoose''. It was in the ''stane hoose'' that Provost Thomas entertained King James V (1513-1542) when he visited the burgh in 1537.

During the year 1538, Thomas Menzies acted as Marischal Depute of Scotland and in 1543 was appointed Comptroller of the Royal Household which probably accounts for the Royal Arms of Scotland being displayed over those of Menzies on the Belmont Street panel. Thomas died in 1576 and a century later his family's name had become a memory in the civic life of Aberdeen. However an echo of their former glories sounded in 1660 when the ''stane hoose'' in the Castlegate was honoured by a visit from Charles II (1660-1685).

By the beginning of the 18th century, the Castlegate house was beginning to show signs of decay and with the projected formation of Marischal Street, John Menzies, the owner of that time, decided to ''ding doon'' the old ''stane hoose'', sell the valuable site fronting the Castlegate, and build himself a smaller, more up-to-date dwelling at the rear of his ''land''. This was done about the year 1740—to designs by the famous architect William Adam of Maryburgh—and so the Menzies' ''back-house'', with its picturesque O-gee gable and finely-moulded chimney-heads, eventually became a well-known feature at the south end of Victoria Court. Unhappily, the ''back-house'' was demolished in 1966 and the final link with the Menzies in the Castlegate broken.

However, as the burgh of Aberdeen gradually expanded— and the tendency was to move westwards—the Menzies secured a property on the west side of a recently formed street off Schoolhill. Formerly known as Caberstone Croft, this land had been acquired in 1778 by George Moir of Scotstown, and on it he erected a dignified mansion-house in the Classical tradition. Now numbered 37 Belmont Street, it passed in 1793 to Moir's son Alexander, and in 1806 was purchased by John Menzies of Pitfodels who subsequently disposed of the Castlegate "back-house". In 1831, No. 37 was acquired by Catherine Burnett, widow of Alexander Forbes of Schivas, who remained in possession until 1848 when it became the headquarters of the Deaf and Dumb Institute. In 1901, the house was occupied by the Gordon Highlanders' Memorial Institute and is now the property of Nicol Smith Company.

The story of the heraldic panel is now complete. When the old "stane hoose" in the Castlegate was demolished in 1766, Thomas Menzies' panel was removed for safe-keeping to John Menzies' "back-house", and when in 1806 the family vacated the "back-house" for their new home at 37 Belmont Street, the old panel was taken along for preservation. Today, it is an interesting reminder of a very remarkable family.

16

CURIOUS HERBAL

"Full many a flow'r is born to blush unseen,
And waste its sweetness on the desert air."
—Thomas Gray.

THE place held by Scotland in the realms of botany must surely be unique—and this despite the vagaries of its climate. For centuries Scottish botanists have been recording and classifying plant life and, curious as it may seem, the north-east corner has probably produced more botanists of international reputation than any other district in the country.

One of these north-east botanists, and quite in a class by herself, was Elizabeth Blackwell. She was a remarkable woman and a typical product of the area—industrious, meticulous and indefatigabie. Her story is as romantic as it is unusual.

In the Aberdeenshire parish of Fyvie, just north of Fyvie Castle, lie the farms of North and South Blachrie. There is nothing unusual about these farms, their claim to mention resting solely on the fact that they took from or gave their name to a family of Blachrie, a number of whom rose to prominence.

Although records show that Blachries were still living in the Fyvie district in 1696, the main stem of the family would appear to have settled in Aberdeen during the latter part of the 15th century. The first to be mentioned is William Blachrie who, about the year 1690, married Isobel Fordyce, a sister of George Fordyce, Provost of Aberdeen in 1717-1719, whose ancestors had been near neighbours of the Blachries in Fyvie.

William Blachrie was a merchant and burgess of trade. He specialised in the stocking industry, then a particularly lucrative business in Aberdeen, and in consequence amassed a very considerable fortune. This enabled Blachrie to provide a liberal education for his sons and substantial marriage portions for his daughters.

In the year 1700, the Rev. Thomas Blackwell (1660-1728) of Paisley—a son of Thomas Blackwell the Covenanter—accepted a call to Aberdeen where he became minister of the town's kirk of St. Nicholas. Eventually, Blackwell was appointed to the Chair of Divinity at Marischal College, Aberdeen, and in 1717 became Principal of the University. The Principal's sister, Elizabeth, had married the Rev. David Brown of Neilston Church, near Paisley, and their daughter Elizabeth became the second wife of the already-mentioned George Fordyce, Provost of Aberdeen. Thus, by marriage, three families became linked—the Blachries, the Fordyces and the Blackwells.[6]

By his wife Christian Johnston, a daughter of Dr. John Johnston, a well-known Glasgow physician, Principal Thomas Blackwell had a family of three—two sons and a daughter. The elder son Thomas (1707-1757), became Professor of Greek at Marischal College and in 1748 was appointed Principal, while the daughter Christian married John French, Advocate in Aberdeen. The second son Alexander (1709-1747) was something of an enigma. As a youth, he conformed to his family's rigid academic pattern but there was much of his Covenanting grandfather's independence and love of freedom in his make-up and these hereditary influences were soon to appear. Consequently, before completing his studies at Marischal College, Alexander Blackwell wooed, eloped with and married his second cousin Elizabeth Blachrie, the sixth daughter of William the stocking merchant. The impact of this run-away marriage on the douce, academic circles of 18th century Aberdeen can well be imagined. The young couple found their way to London.

The next we hear of Alexander Blackwell is in Leyden studying medicine under Hermann Boerhaave, the celebrated physician and botanist. It would seem that Elizabeth Blachrie accompanied her husband to Leyden where, according to Blackwell himself, he graduated in medicine. However, in 1728, Blackwell was back in London—not practising as a physician as one might expect—but acting as proof-reader in the establishment of Wilkins, a well-known printer.

In 1730, Alexander Blackwell set up as a printer on his own account in the Strand but appears to have met with bitter opposition from the printing trade ring and in consequence became involved in debt. Blackwell was committed to Highgate Prison for two years. At this juncture, his remarkable wife Elizabeth Blachrie—described as "an ingenious lady"—rose to prominence. She resolved to clear her husband's debts and secure his release.

While living in Aberdeen, Elizabeth had received some training in drawing and painting at which she had shown more than average ability. She had also developed, along with her brother Alexander—later a surgeon in Bromley, Kent —a keen interest in botany. Elizabeth Blachrie now determined to put her talents to use. Accordingly, she made a series of drawings of various herbs used in medicine and these she submitted to Sir Hans Sloane and Dr. Richard Mead, eminent physicians of the day. Both men were much impressed by her work and urged her to continue with a view to publication. Elizabeth then took lodgings near Chelsea Botanical Gardens where she obtained all the plants necessary for her project. It was an enormous task, for she made all the drawings of the plants, engraved the plates and coloured every print by hand.

The first volume of Elizabeth Blackwell's work was published in 1737 under the title *A Curious Herbal: containing Five Hundred Cuts of the most useful plants which are now used in the Practise of Physick*. A second volume appeared in 1739. The *Herbal* was an immediate and phenomenal success and so highly was it rated by the medical profession that editions were subsequently published in Nuremberg and Leipzig. With the proceeds from the sale of the *Herbal*, Elizabeth Blackwell secured her husband's release from Highgate Prison. Yet, despite the amazing success of her publication, Elizabeth's troubles were by no means over.

On his release from Highgate, Alexander Blackwell obtained an introduction to James Brydges, Duke of Chandos, who immediately recognised Blackwell's genius and appointed him Director of Improvements at Canons Park, Edgeware, Middlesex—sold as a housing estate in 1929. Eventually, Blackwell went to Sweden where in 1742 he was appointed Physician-in-Ordinary to King Frederick. It then seemed as if Blackwell's position was at long last secure.

However, as time passed, Alexander Blackwell became immensely popular with Frederick and his influence with the king aroused the jealousy of the Swedish ministers, particularly the powerful Count Tessin. As a result, just as Elizabeth Blackwell was preparing to leave London to join her husband in Sweden, he himself, by a cunning political manipulation, was accused of treason, subjected to torture and condemned to death. He was sentenced to be broken on the wheel but this was later commuted to decapitation and so, on 9th August, 1747, Alexander Blackwell was executed.[7]

Following upon this great tragedy, Elizabeth Blackwell completely disappears. It is presumed she died in London but the date and her place of burial are unknown. A heroic woman, Elizabeth Blackwell's only memorial is her work *A Curious Herbal*, now quite rare.

Facing.   1. Chapel Court, Justice Street.
2. Arms of Thomas Menzies, Belmont Street.

1

2

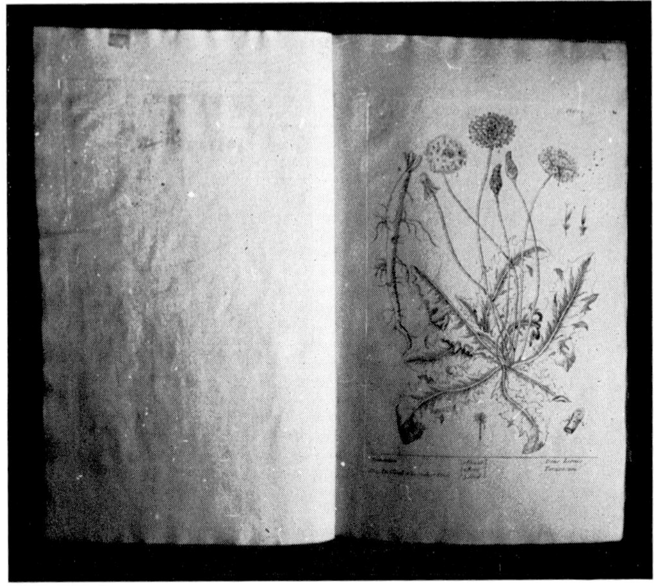

1

2

3

17

TALE OF THE TOLBOOTH

"Opportunity makes a thief."
—Francis Bacon.

ABERDEEN'S Tolbooth—of old referred to as "The Mids o' Mar"—is undoubtedly one of the most fascinating buildings in the city. Most people who visit the grim old tower with its iron-bound doors, massive bolts, chains and padlocks, frequently pose the question "Did anybody ever escape from here?" It certainly seems improbable, yet the answer is "yes", for one young man—Peter Young—actually escaped from the condemned cell and tiptoed to freedom through the front door of the building. His life-story is the stuff of thrillers, gangster films and television serials.

Peter Young belonged to a notorious band of gypsies whose "territory" included the whole of north-east Scotland from the Firth of Forth to the Moray coast. The headquarters of the band was at Lochgelly in Fife where John Gunn, the last of Rob Roy MacGregor's henchmen, reigned as "king". However, Gunn subsequently exiled himself and the gypsy "kingship" passed to Charles "Gle'ed" Graham— "squint-eyed" Graham—a skilled horner and spoon-maker. This "Gle'ed" Graham had an only sister Ann who married James "Caird" Young—"Gypsy" Young—and by him had three sons, Robert, Peter and John, the second being the subject of this story.

Facing.   1. A Curious Herbal (vol. 1).
        2. Doorway, condemned cell in Tolbooth.
        3. Aberdeen's Tolbooth, Lodge Walk.

F

Peter Young was born in 1764 but his birthplace is not recorded. However, as Peter regarded himself a Deeside man, it seems probable that he was born in the remote gypsy hide-out known as "Red-beard's Cave" in the Kincardineshire parish of Durris, where his family were known to "lurk" and where Peter frequently hid in times of stress.[8]

Peter's early life was spent with his parents moving about from place to place within the gypsy "territory". Of course he had no schooling and could neither read nor write although he possessed amazing powers of concentration. Like all gypsies, Peter was skilled in woodcraft, had remarkable agility, was an expert tinker and metal-worker—and a very clever pickpocket. In addition, Peter possessed initiative, had a flair for disguise and was endowed with unusual cunning.

Peter Young is first heard of in the Aberdeenshire parish of Tough where at the age of fifteen he bungled his first "break-in" job and was lucky to escape with a thrashing. Equally unfortunate was his second job which he did in collaboration with his elder brother Robert when both were caught and sent to Aberdeen to be "made over" to the Army. They were lodged in the Tolbooth and here Peter's amazing ingenuity showed itself for the first time. He concocted a a paste which he and his brother smeared on their bodies. They then reported an outbreak of scurvy and were immediately removed to hospital. Here, escape was easy, and having regained their freedom, Peter and Robert wisely decided to part company.

Peter Young now went south to seek his fortune—and nearly found it—for he successfully pulled off a burglary in York and got away. With some money in his pocket, Peter next set sail on a privateer but the vessel was captured and we next hear of him in America serving with Washington's Light Horse. From this time onwards, Peter's career is indeed a chequered one for he was successively soldier, buccaneer, sailor, brigand and state prisoner. However, in 1782, he returned to north-east Scotland at the age of eighteen.

Shortly after his return, Peter married his cousin Jean Wilson and although their life together was tragically short, it was a true love-match. Young's escapades had already become legendary but the sands were rapidly running out and there was obviously only one end to his fantastic career of crime.

Eventually, for thefts they had committed in Banff, Portsoy and other towns, Peter and Jean were apprehended and imprisoned in Turriff. Once again they escaped but were soon recaptured and sent under military guard to Aberdeen for trial. Both were found guilty and condemned to death by hanging. The execution was fixed for 16th November, 1787, but as Jean was expecting their first child, the date of her execution was postponed until after its birth.

On this occasion, Peter was lodged in the condemned cell of the Tolbooth where leg-irons secured him to the floor of the grim, vaulted apartment. Escape now seemed impossible. Yet Peter's ingenuity once more prevailed and with the help of two "outside" contacts, an unbelievable break-out involving Peter, his wife Jean, and all the other prisoners in the Tolbooth, was made in the early hours of 25th October. By nightfall they were safe in the Durris hide-out.

But the end was now in sight. Before long, all the fugitives were retaken and when Peter Young arrived in Aberdeen on New Year's Day, 1788, he was given a tremendous welcome by the citizens. However, fearing that Peter's popularity might be the means of his making yet another "break-out", the magistrates had him secretly removed under cover of darkness and conveyed to Edinburgh where he was placed in a specially-made iron cage within the condemned cell of the "Heart of Midlothian".

Thus, after a protracted trial, Peter Young was again found guilty and condemned to death. At the age of twenty-four he was hanged in Edinburgh on Wednesday, 2nd July, 1788, and on the day of the execution his wife Jean gave birth to their child in the Tolbooth at Aberdeen. Less than a month later, she walked the short distance from the prison to the gibbet in the Castlegate where her young life ended.

18

PROVOSTS, PORTRAITS AND POLITICS

"Aince a Provost, aye my Lord."
—Charles Murray.

ALTHOUGH the names of Aberdeen's provosts are on record from the year 1272, portraits of its early civic heads are relatively few. The first of these portraits dates from the 15th century. They are tomb-effigies, the earliest being that of Robert Davidson who fell at the battle of Harlaw in 1411 during his term of office as provost.

Davidson's effigy, which is preserved in Collison's Aisle, St. Nicholas Church, is somewhat mutilated and in consequence loses some of its value as a portrait. However, the effigy does give an excellent idea of the armour worn by Davidson on the battlefield and shows what is probably the provost's chain of office. According to custom, Davidson's head rests on his helmet and it is interesting to note he is wearing a "quoif" of the period—the small crimson cap which was found on his skull three centuries after the provost's death when his remains were accidentally uncovered in Collison's Aisle.

A full century elapses before we find another portrait of a provost, Gilbert Menzies, and by good fortune he is accompanied by his lady. Both these portraits are tomb-effigies and, like that of Provost Davidson, are preserved in St. Nicholas Church although the tomb they originally adorned is some miles distant.

The story now moves to Kincardineshire—to the village of Findon, some eight miles south from Aberdeen. Anciently known as Auchinvyok, Findon has been from a very early period closely associated with the civic life of Aberdeen. Three successive owners of Findon were provosts—William de Camera (Chalmers), John Vaus and Gilbert Menzies who acquired the property in 1539.

The son of David Menzies of the Pitfodels family by his wife Margaret Fotheringham, Gilbert Menzies of Findon—known to his contemporaries as "Banison Gib"—was a member of the celebrated family whose collective occupancy of Aberdeen's civic chair totalled one hundred and thirty years. Gilbert himself served no less than six terms as provost covering a period of twenty-five years. His first term began in 1505 while his last year in office was 1536.

On looking over the records of the time when Gilbert Menzies was provost, the similarity between the Town Council's deliberations of four hundred years ago and those of today is quite remarkable. For example, we find the Council dealing with such items as public health, streets and roads, trade and shop-keepers' hours, fishing, defence and entertainment—even party politics in civic affairs were not unknown in the 16th century.

Like our Lord Provosts of today, Gilbert Menzies of Findon was a very busy man. He presided at meetings, attended functions such as the opening of the Bridge of Dee, and welcomed Royalty—in 1511 Margaret Tudor, Queen of James IV (1488-1513), visited Aberdeen. As frequently happens with Royal visits, this one had its problems. The gift of £200 Scots. made to the Queen by the magistrates required some "cooking" in the treasurer's accounts. However, records indicate that the difficulty was resolved in the usual way—an increase on the rates. Literally, no stone was left unturned in order to create a a good impression on the Royal visitor and all "myddings" were ordered to be removed from the Shiprow and other main streets lest their "awfu' stynk" should assail the Queen's nostrils.

Gilbert Menzies of Findon married Marjory, daughter of Provost Alexander de Camera, by whom he had five sons and a daughter. In 1535, Menzies acquired the lands of Maryculter from the Knights of St. John of Jerusalem and when he died in 1543 the provost was buried in the Knight's chapel of St. Mary at Maryculter. His wife Marjory ''departit this lyf'' in 1553 and was interred alongside her busband. Effigies of the provost and his lady were erected over their tomb which remained tolerably entire until the middle of last century. Eventually, however, to preserve them from the ravages of time and weather, the effigies were removed from Maryculter to the West Church of St. Nicholas in Aberdeen, a fitting refuge for the relics of a worthy provost and his lady.

19

"THE GUIDIN' O'T"

"To have found favour with leaders of Mankind
is not the meanest of glories."
—Horace.

THE number of Scotsmen who have been compelled to leave their native land to seek fame and fortune in other climes must surely be unique in the annals of any country of comparable size. Religious, political or economic reasons, sometimes all three, have usually been the cause for emigration, thus "the Scot abroad" has become almost a legendary figure in world history. J. M. Barrie aptly puts it—*"There are few more impressive sights in the world than a Scotsman on the make"*.

There cannot be many lands but have, at one time or another, benefitted from a Scottish "invasion" and it is interesting to recall the influence exercised by a quartette of north-east men in Russia where their sway continued for more than a century. Typical of their kind, these "Scoto-Russians" were Patrick Gordon (1635-1699), Thomas Gordon (1658-1714), James Francis Edward Keith (1696-1758), and Michael Andreas Barclay (1761-1818).

A Buchan "loon", Patrick Gordon was born in 1635 at East Auchleuchries in the Aberdeenshire parish of Cruden. He was the son of John Gordon of Auchleuchries and his wife Mary Ogilvie who, like so many of their illustrious House, were staunch Roman Catholics. As a youth, Patrick attended the village school at Cruden and the parish school at Ellon, his intention being to enter a university. However, problems of religion arose and at the age of sixteen he set sail from Aberdeen for Danzig. Patrick then proceeded to East Prussia where he entered the Jesuit College at Braunsberg. For two years he remained at college but the tranquil, almost monastic life imposed there did not suit Patrick's active temperament and in 1653 he gave up his studies planning to return to Scotland. However, fate—which was to play such an important part in Patrick Gordon's career—intervened. No ship could be found sailing for Scotland.

He then tried to enlist in a Scottish regiment of the Polish Army but was unsuccessful. However, he became companion to a young Polish nobleman whom he accompanied to Hamburg, his intention being to sail for Scotland. While waiting for a ship, Patrick fell in with a Rittmaster Garden—probably of Aberdeen extraction—who was enlisting recruits for Gustavus Adolphus of Sweden. Before long, Gordon was a cavalryman in the Swedish Army on its way to invade Poland.

In the true tradition of the Scottish soldier-of-fortune of the period, Gordon changed sides several times during the next few years—sometimes he was in the Swedish Army as often in the Polish. Eventually, in 1616, peace came between the two countries and again Patrick had thoughts of returning home, for the restoration of Charles II had taken place. A letter from his father dissuaded him and in July, 1661, Patrick went to Riga and so to Moscow where he joined the Russian Army of Tsar Alexis with the rank of major. This proved to be the turning point in his career. The following year, Gordon was promoted lieutenant-colonel and married Catherine von Bockhoven, the daughter of a Russian colonel.

The year 1665 saw him in London on a mission from the Tsar. There he was cordially received by Charles II and made many friends at Court, among them the Earl of Erroll, whose Aberdeenshire estates adjoined Auchleuchries. The following year he returned to Russia where his regiment was serving in the Ukraine. In 1682 his wife died and some years later he married a lady of Dutch extraction. Gordon was promoted lieutenant-general in 1683.

By this time, his father John Gordon of Auchleuchries and his elder brother had died. At length—in February 1686—Patrick obtained leave of absence to return to Scotland in order to settle up his family affairs and on this occasion was fêted by the magistrates of Aberdeen. He visited Auchleuchries and spent a night at Haddo House as guest of the Earl of Aberdeen. Patrick returned to Moscow in July and the following year was promoted general. However, his appointment drew censure from the Russian Orthodox Church whose patriach prophesied disaster to the Russian Army if commanded by a heretic. It was a difficult time for Gordon but he had attracted the attention of young Prince Peter—later to be Peter "the Great"—who finally appointed him rear-admiral of the Russian Fleet at Archangel. In 1697, the Tsar visited Great Britain and Gordon was left as second in command of Russia's military might. Two years later, his health began to decline and on 29th November, 1699, Patrick Gordon died at the age of sixty-four—Tsar Peter remaining at his bedside to the end. He was buried in Moscow.

Patrick Gordon has been described as "the perfect type of military adventurer of the 17th century, a brave, capable man, full of resource, but ready to transfer his services to the cause which paid him best".

The second member of the Scoto-Russian quartette was Thomas Gordon. Born in Aberdeen in 1658, he was the son of Dr. Thomas Gordon and his wife Jean Hay. He received his early education at Aberdeen Grammar School, but having determined on a maritime career, went off to sea when quite young.

The first notice regarding Thomas Gordon's career is dated 1693. On 28th February of that year, he received a Royal Warrant to sail from Campvere—the port of the Scottish merchants in the Netherlands—to the Mediterranean as captain on the privateer *Margaret* of Aberdeen, with its complement of a hundred men and thirty guns.

From subsequent records, it would seem that Gordon soon made his mark as a "merchant captain" but this did not satisfy him and he eventually gravitated to the Scottish Navy. In 1703, he is mentioned as being in command of the *Royal Mary*.

It appears that he had become involved in the Jacobite intrigue of the time, and it is recorded that on 11th August, 1707, the *Royal Mary* was lying off the Buchan coast of Aberdeenshire where Gordon received "certain intelligence" from Slains Castle, the residence of the Erroll family. Gordon seems to have acted as a Jacobite agent on several occasions.

However, on 1st May, 1707, the Scottish Navy had been taken over by the English Admiralty and eight years later, the year of the Jacobite Rising, Thomas Gordon was required to take the Oath of Allegiance to George I. He declined to do so. Thereafter, Gordon either resigned his Commission or was dismissed from the Navy for his Jacobite sympathies. He then went to the Netherlands where he had many friends and it was here that Gordon met Tsar Peter of Russia, then planning the formation of a Russian Navy.

The Tsar immediately assessed Gordon's worth and so, two years later, we find the Scotsman in the role of rear-admiral of the Russian Navy. From that date onwards, Gordon more than fulfilled the Tsar's expectations. In 1725, he was appointed admiral of the Russian Fleet and invested with the Order of St. Alexander Nevsky with Red Ribbon. These honours were followed in 1732 by the presentation to him of the Delegate's House at Kronstadt as a hereditary freehold estate, and in 1733 he was appointed Governor of Kronstadt for life.

Admiral Gordon visited Scotland in 1736 and in June of that year was made an Honorary Burgess of Aberdeen. He returned to Russia and died in 1741 having completed nearly a quarter of a century in the Russian Navy.

James Francis Edward Keith was the third member of the quartette to find fame in Russia. Born on 11th June,

1696, he was the second son of William Keith, 9th Earl Marischal, and his wife Lady Maria Drummond, daughter of the Earl of Perth. He was educated privately and subsequently studied law at Edinburgh University. An ardent Jacobite, he joined the ill-starred Rising of 1715, took part in several of the engagements, and after Sheriffmuir succeeded in escaping to Brittany.

About the age of twenty, Keith endeavoured to enlist in the service of both Russia and Sweden but was unsuccessful. In 1719 he took part in the abortive Jacobite expedition to the Western Highlands and again escaped taking ship from Peterhead to Texel in Holland, eventually making his way to Paris and Rome. By the year 1720 he was in Madrid —a colonel in the Spanish Army. However, as a devout Episcopalian, Keith realised that his chances of promotion in Roman Catholic Spain were nil, so with the active support of the Duke of Liria—son of the Duke of Berwick, natural son of James II of Great Britain—then Spanish ambassador in Moscow, he entered the Russian Army with the rank of major. His advancement was rapid — in 1730 lieutenant-colonel and two years later inspector general of the army on the Volga and Don.

In the Russian war against Turkey, he was appointed general of infantry and at the storming of Otchakoff in July, 1737, was severely wounded in the knee. His wound did not heal and his brother, now Earl Marischal of Scotland, travelled from Spain to be at his side. He insisted that Keith be taken to Paris for treatment and on passing through Prussia, the brothers were warmly received by King Frederick William and the Crown Prince. In Paris, the cause of his suffering was discovered and the wound healed so satisfactorily that he was able to travel to London where, despite his continued Jacobite sympathies, he was cordially received by George II.

Keith was urgently recalled to Russia on account of the outbreak of the war with Sweden. This campaign was entirely successful and when Keith returned in 1744 he was richly rewarded by the Empress Elizabeth. However, his dazzling success raised indignation among the Russians and gradually his commands and appointments were reduced. Feeling that continued residence in Russia was bringing him dangerously near to banishment in Siberia, Keith quietly slipped away—to Prussia where within a month, King Frederick appointed him field-marshal of the Prussian Army. Two years later, he was made Governor of Berlin.

While taking part in the disastrous engagement at Hochkirch on 14th August, 1758, James Francis Edward Keith was killed in the thick of the fighting. The Austrians buried him in the village church at Hochkirch with full military honours, but three months later, King Frederick had his remains removed to the Garrison Church at Berlin. Keith never married. He left his modest estate to his young, attractive mistress Eva Nerthens—a prisoner from the Swedish campaign —whom he had carefully educated and by whom he had several children.

The last member of the quartette was Michael Andreas Barclay. In the year 1621, Sir Patrick Barclay, baron of the barony of Towie in the Aberdeenshire parish of Auchterless, granted a letter of safe-conduct to his two kinsmen, John and Peter Barclay of Banff, who wished to proceed to Livonia in Russia to engage in business. John eventually settled in Norway while Peter became a silk-merchant in Rostock where he married Angela von Vohrden. The great-great-grandson of this union was Michael Andreas Barclay, usually styled as ''de Tollie'' (i.e. ''of Towie'').

At the early age of seven, Michael was entered as a corporal in the Novotroitsky Cuirassier Regiment in which he was eventually promoted to the rank of coronet. The outstanding ability of young Barclay—or Bogdanovich as he was called in Russia—was noted by his commander and in 1788 he was appointed adjutant to Prince Anhalt-Bernburgsky. Barclay served with distinction through several campaigns and was decorated with the Order of St. George.

In 1810, Barclay was appointed Russia's Minister of War and it was during his term of office that the famous Administration of a Great Active Army was established. This was to prove of inestimable value in the Napoleonic wars which lay ahead.

Napoleon invaded Russia and in 1812 Michael Barclay was given command of the main Russian forces. Realising Napoleon's superior strength, Barclay avoided decisive action by ordering a retiral into the depths of the country. His policy was to draw the enemy on letting them gain ground but leaving nothing of value behind. Actually, Barclay was the originator of "the scorched earth policy" used with such success against Germany in the Second World War—for he burned towns and villages, destroyed crops and drove off cattle leaving nothing of value behind. In this way he hoped to break up Napoleon's armies but Russia's military hierarchy demanded a decisive battle and the Tsar reluctantly relieved Barclay of his command. Kutuzov took over and the useless battle of Borodino followed. Finally, however, Kutuzov was obliged to return to Barclay's "scorched earth policy" and Napoleon's armies were shattered. Barclay and his policy were vindicated.

For his remarkable services to Russia, Michael Andreas Barclay was created Prince Barclay de Tollie of the Russian Empire. He accompanied Tsar Alexander I to London in 1814 but there is nothing to suggest he visited his ancestral home in Aberdeenshire—Towie-Barclay Castle near Turriff. Barclay's health deteriorated very quickly after the London visit and he died in 1818 at Insterburg on his way to the German spas.

Thus four north-east men, in their various spheres of activity, served faithfully and well the land of their adoption.

20

F R I E N D V I L L E

"Old houses mended,
Cost little less than new before they're mended."
—Colley Cibber.

IN any expanding city, it is inevitable that some fine old houses once located outwith its boundaries should one day become absorbed by the spreading community. Thus, in their sometimes incongruous urban settings, these fascinating old houses are seen standing alone, like some proud sentinel, jealously guarding the dignity of a bygone age.

The city of Aberdeen is still fortunate in possessing a small number of such buildings—the former homes of county families, of prominent citizens, or of prosperous burgesses. One of the most interesting of these is "Friendville", at the western Mannofield end of Great Western Road. Fortunately, its character has been carefully preserved so that today it is one of the most complete examples of its period in Scotland.

"Friendville" originally formed part of the ancient barony of Rubislaw which, in the 14th century, was described as lying two miles west from the burgh of Aberdeen. In 1359, the barony was possessed by one, John de Inchcur, dominus de Rubislaw, but it would appear to have reverted to the Crown shortly after this date for in 1379 Rubislaw was granted to the Royal burgh of Aberdeen by Robert II (1371-1390).

This grant was signed by Robert on 20th August, 1379, at "Kyndrocht in Marre"—Kindrochit in Braemar. Thereafter, the magistrates of Aberdeen leased the barony to successive "tacksmen", the first being Simon de Camera (Chalmers) of Norman descent, whose family played a leading part in the early civic life of Aberdeen. Simon was "tackman" of Rubislaw in 1498.

About the year 1551, the barony of Rubislaw was feued by the magistrates to Robert Forbes, a cadet of the noble House of Forbes. The Forbeses held the property until 1687 when it was sold by Thomas Forbes of Rubislaw to Sir George Skene, Provost of Aberdeen from 1676 to 1684. It was during the lairdship of Sir George's successor, George Skene, 4th of Rubislaw, that "Friendville" came into being.

In the year 1772, a charter was granted in favour of Robert Balmanno, merchant in Aberdeen, conveying to him part of the barony of Rubislaw. At that time, the land in question was designated "the Inclosures" as it was presumably a fenced area lying within the stretch of desolate country which, on early maps of the district, is called "the foul muirs". Eventually, "the Inclosures" became known as "Balmanno's fields"—later contracted to "Mannofield"—and it was here that Robert Balmanno built his house in 1773 and which, on account of his Quaker ancestry, he subsequently called "Friendville".

The miniature estate of "Friendville" would seem to have included the area of land bounded on the south by Great Western Road, on the west by Countesswells Road, on the north by Seafield Road and Cromwell Road, and on the east by Burns Road. From this area, successive proprietors sold off various portions of "Friendville", the first being "Louisville", then "Wellbrae" and so down the years until 1893 when the last portion later known as "Thorngrove" was detached, leaving "Friendville" with $2\frac{1}{4}$ acres.

In 1790, Robert Balmanno, who belonged to the ancient Balmanno family of that ilk, sold "Friendville" to Arthur Dingwall-Fordyce of Culsh, Commissary of Aberdeen. During his short time as proprietor, Balmanno did much to improve the land and several of the grand old trees in Seafield Road and Thorngrove Aveune were planted by him. Records tell that fully five acres were "under strawberries which supplied the London markets". In 1802, Arthur Dingwall-Fordyce disposed of the property to his brother-in-law the Rev. James Sherriffs, minister of the West Kirk of St. Nicholas, Aberdeen, and Patron of the Incorporated Trades, whose portrait hangs in Trinity Hall, Aberdeen.

The Rev. James Sherriffs was one of four remarkable brothers—sons of David Sherriffs, a prosperous Aberdeen carpenter. The other sons were Alexander, Advocate in Aberdeen, proprietor of "Louisville"; Andrew, poet and editor of *The Caledonian Magazine* whom Robert Burns succinctly described after their meeting in 1787 as "a little decrepit body with some abilities"; and David who accumu-lated a very considerable fortune as a planter in Jamaica. On David's death, his fortune eventually devolved on his brother James of "Friendville" who not only succeeded to the "siller" but also to one hundred and sixty-two able-bodied negro slaves, seventy-seven male and eighty-five female—surely an embarrassing legacy for a minister of the Church of Scotland and Moderator of the General Assembly.

The Sherriffs remained at "Friendville" until 1830 when the property passed by marriage to Robert Burnett, a cadet of the Burnett family of Leys in Kincardineshire. Ten years later, "Friendville" was purchased from the Burnetts by a family of Mackenzies from Bombay who in 1893 sold it to William Jackson who later built "Thorngrove" for his own occupation—the first house in Aberdeen to be lit by electricity. In 1917, the property was acquired by A. T. Cruickshank,

Facing. 1. Tomb effigies, West Church of St. Nicholas.

2. General Patrick Gordon.

3. Admiral Thomas Gordon.

4. Field Marshall Keith.

5. Prince Barclay de Tollie.

1

2

3

4

5

1

GEORGE DAVID
SONE ELDER BVRGES
OF ABD. BIGIT THIS
DVK ON HIS OVIN
EXPENSES 1650

2

Advocate in Aberdeen, and in 1934 "Friendville" was purchased by William S. Bell, antique dealer.

The mansion-house of "Friendville" is typical of the
period to which it belongs. As already mentioned, it was
erected by Robert Balmanno in the year 1773 and in its
original state consisted of a simple, rectangular house of two
floors and a garret. Projecting from the house on the north
front was a small, one-storey wing containing the kitchen.
However, in the year 1812, this kitchen wing was enlarged
to provide additional accommodation and a carved stone,
built into the east wall, commemorates the undertaking. It
bears the initials J. S. and A. M.—the Rev. James Sherriffs
and his wife Amelia Morison, daughter of Provost James
Morison of Elsick, and sister of the Rev. George Morison of
Banchory-Devenick, builder of the well-known "Shakkin'
Briggie" at Cults—and the date 1812.

The house is built of squared and dressed granite, doubtless surface gatherings from the site, which gives the buliding
a particularly pleasing colour and texture. Its main front,
with the attractive gablet and semi-circular-headed window,
is full of charm and possesses the simple, well-proportioned
dignity which marked such domestic bulidings during the 18th
century. Today, it is difficult to appreciate that in 1792,
"Friendville" was described as possessing "a fine view of the
town, bay and harbour, also the river and bridge of Dee".

It goes without saying, that "Friendville" was altered and
added to by its various owners. However, in 1952, another
chapter was added to its fascinating story when the building
was restored to its original form and its garden laid out in
the formal style of the 18th century. "Friendville" now
holds much of unusual interest. For example, its entrance
gateway is by Warren, the celebrated 18th century wrought-
iron worker, and once graced the old Grange at North End,
Kensington, London, the home of Sir Edward Burne-Jones,
R.A., the famous artist. The charming Ionic belvedere in

Facing. 1. Friendville, Mannofield.

2. Davidson's plaque, East St. Clement's church-yard.

G

sandstone with its wrought-iron dome—the main feature of
the front lawn—originally stood in the grounds of Ashley
Park, Walton-on-Thames, Surrey. These and many other
interesting items, many of them of international importance,
makes "Friendville" unique in Scotland.

It is heartening to know that, within the busy commercial
city of Aberdeen, there stands such a house, redolent of the
past and possessing all the charm and tranquility of a bygone
age—the embodiment of its name "Friendville". In the rush
and turmoil of today, the deep-cut motto over its entrance
doorway is surely significant—the first line of the quaint old
Scottish proverb—

"Tak' tent o' Time,
Ere Time be tint".

21

PACKMAN'S PENCE

"If money go before, all ways do lie open."
—Shakespeare.

ABERDEENSHIRE has long been noted for its self-made men—people of humble origin who, by hard and unremitting labour, have built up vast fortunes thus securing for themselves a position of power in the community. Many such have come and gone, for as a general rule, their memory fades with death.

One of the most remarkable of these self-made men was George Davidson of Pettens, an indefatigable worker and public benefactor, yet possessed of an odd streak of vanity—a desire to be "somebody", to be regarded as a scholar and revered by posterity.

Curiously enough, George Davidson's origin is as obscure as his date of birth. He was said to be connected with the Davidson family of Cairnbrogie in the parish of Tarves, and this is possible—perhaps he was born on the wrong side of the blanket, thus producing a psychological basis for his tremendous drive and thirst for recognition. He is believed to have been born in the latter years of the 16th century but his parentage is unknown and whether he deliberately concealed this or whether he did not know who his parents were, is uncertain. He had a "sister" and three "brothers"—one of them younger than himself and also called George—all five being equally silent as to his parentage. Nevertheless, whatever the mystery of his origin may be, it would seem that very early in life George Davidson developed an insatiable desire for fame and fortune. It was obvious that the only way to achieve this ambition was by acquiring great wealth but as he had no schooling and could neither read nor write, his chances of success seemed small indeed. He had one great asset, however—he "kent the richt side o' a bawbee".

As a youth, Davidson started up in business as a packman, a pedlar, whose "territory" included the whole of Scotland's north-east corner. This area he covered entirely on foot, working long hours and saving every penny he made. In this way—with some money-lending on the side—George laid the foundation of his fortune. By the year 1626 he was sufficiently affluent to be admitted a burgess of Aberdeen and some four years later he settled permanently in the city, being now well on the way to becoming "somebody".

In 1631, George Davidson was in a position to make his first public benefaction. This was to old Fittie Kirk—now East St. Clement's Church—which, since the Reformation, had fallen into disrepair. A fund was opened for its restoration and Davidson was one of the subscribers.

The opportunity to enhance his social position came in 1643 when Davidson acquired the lands of Pettens in the parish of Belhelvie. The price paid for Pettens was 16,224 merks, yet within the next few years, Davidson added the lands of Westburn, Bogfairly and Kepplehills—later called Newhills—to his possessions. He was now referred to as George Davidson of Pettens, thus achieving his ambition to be "somebody".

In 1650, Davidson made a second gift to Fittie Kirk—a great, stone-built boundary wall which to this day encloses the ancient grave-yard. Here, on the north wall, may still be seen the much-weathered tablet commemorating the gift—

"George Davidson, elder,
burgess of Aberdonensis,
bigit this dyke
on his own expenses"

This tablet is interesting on two points. First, the word
"elder", here used to distinguish George from his younger
"brother" of the same name, and second, the coat of arms
displayed below the inscription for it poses the question—had
George Davidson of Pettens the legal right to armorial bearings or was it a piece of vanity?   Several local historians have
explained its presence as "proof" of Davidson's connection with the Cairnbrogie family.   However, this cannot be
accepted for the arms on the tablet are not those of Davidson
of Cairnbrogie, and furthermore, there is no record in the
Ordinary of Scottish Arms that George Davidson of Pettens
ever received a heraldic grant.

Be that as it may, George Davidson's substantial gifts and
mortifications to the parish of Newhills are his real memorials
and they endure to the present time.   His bridge over the
Buck's Burn at Bucksburn and his bridge at Insch were
obviously the gestures of a generous heart as were his various
mortifications to the Kirk of St. Nicholas in Aberdeen.

George Davidson of Pettens died in the year 1663 and was
buried near "the West Kirk style of St. Nicholas".   Here,
his massive headstone vies in grandeur with any in the kirkyard, yet it seems curious that this impressive memorial with
its lengthy Latin inscription should commemorate a simple
"packman chiel" who could neither read nor write his own
language—and it is interesting to note that the niche for his
coat of arms is void.   One wonders why?

22

FORGOTTEN FORMER PUPIL

"Bon Record."
—Aberdeen Grammar School motto.

HAD John Knox, the celebrated reformer, any connection with north-east Scotland?   History tells he was born at Giffordgate, a suburb of Haddington, but very little is known of his ancestry except what Knox himself records as having said to the infamous Earl of Bothwell—"my grandfather, grandsire, and father have served under your lordship's predecessors, and some of them have died under their standards".   One is therefore left guessing—where did the Knox family originate?

"The aspect of the Reformation in Aberdeen exhibited nothing peculiar" is how one noted historian describes the city's reaction to this historic event in Scottish history.   It is recorded that the citizens resolutely refused to "ding doon" the parish kirk of St. Nicholas yet, ever practical, had no objections to the "rouping" of the church plate and vestments nor to the proceeds from their sale being directed towards the cost of a new bulwark at the harbour.   The real damage, we are told, and the horrible murder of Brother Francis were the work of "Knox's rabble" from the south (see Chapter 11).

However, it was in Aberdeen that the first murmurings of the Reformation were heard in 1521—in the Grammar School—when John Marshall, a young master there, was summoned to appear before the provost and magistrates to answer for his contempt of the Church. For two years, Marshall was persecuted for his advanced views but eventually he recanted and received the magistrates' pardon. The Reformation came in 1560.

The years passed and in 1622 a "new boy" entered the Aberdeen Grammar School. This was Nathaniel Welch, third son of the Rev. John Welch, minister of Ayr. The "new boy" was boarded with the rector of the school, David Wedderburn, who was awarded "four score of pounds Scots quarterly" by the Town Council of Aberdeen for the "bedding, buirding and the washing of the said Nathaniel his claiths". This Nathaniel Welch was the grandson of John Knox, the reformer.

It will be recalled that John Knox was twice married: firstly when he was forty-eight years old to Marjorie Bowes— then barely eighteen—the fifth daughter of Sir Robert Bowes of Norham Castle, Northumberland—by whom he had two sons, Nathaniel and Eleaser. Secondly, John Knox when close on sixty years of age, married Margaret, the fifteen year old daughter of Andrew Stewart, 3rd Lord Ochiltree. Ochiltree was directly descended from Robert II (1371-1390) and was "of the blood" of Scotland's Royal House. Thus Knox's marriage to a Stewart was a bitter blow to Mary Queen of Scots.

By his child-wife Margaret Stewart, the reformer had a family of three daughters—Martha, Margaret and Elizabeth, the latter marrying in 1594, the Rev. John Welch, minister of Ayr, by whom she had three sons and two daughters. The third son was Nathaniel, who attended Aberdeen Grammar School as a boarder from 1622 to 1626.

Nathaniel Welch came to the Grammar School in the year of his father's death and his mother died during his sojourn at school. Left an orphan, Nathaniel eventually went to sea and was shipwrecked but managed to save himself by swimming to a rocky island. There, for lack of food and water, Nathaniel died and when his body was discovered some considerable time later, it was found in an attitude of prayer.

The reason why Aberdeen Grammar School should have been selected for Nathaniel Welch has never been explained. It would seem that neither of his parents' families had any Aberdeen connections, yet the Town Council defrayed all the boy's expenses during his four years' stay in the burgh.

However, it is just possible that the Knox family originated in north-east Scotland. In 1472, Andrew Knox of that ilk is mentioned in a charter—he held the lands of Knox some 10 miles west from Peterhead—while in 1498 the name of David Knox of Auchorthy in the Aberdeenshire parish of Strichen, appears in witness to a document. At all events, in the parish of Old Deer, near the ruins of the famous Abbey, is the property from which the family derived their name— Knox, today spelt Knock.

23

WHEN A DUCHESS KISS'D

"There's a yellow thread in the Gordon plaid,
But it binds na my love an' me;
And the ivy leaf has brought dool and grief
Where there never but love should be."
—Charles Murray.

THE story of the raising of the Gordon Highlanders is a curious mixture of fact and fiction, for a picturesque legend is often more acceptable than the simple truth. The actual raising of the Regiment, however, was the particular concern of three people for, according to records of the time, they "recruited in their own person"—Alexander, 4th Duke of Gordon (1743-1827), his wife Jane Maxwell (1748-1812), and their son George, Marquis of Huntly (1770-1836). Thus the early history of the Gordon Highlanders is closely interwoven with the lives of these three fascinating characters, now almost forgotten except, of course, for the Duchess Jean whose unique place in the legendary lore of the Regiment is assured.

Alexander, 4th Duke of Gordon, was born at Gordon Castle, Fochabers, in the year 1743. He was the eldest son of Cosmo George, 3rd Duke of Gordon (1720-1752), by his wife the Lady Catherine Gordon, second daughter of his brother-in-law William, 2nd Earl of Aberdeen. The Florentine name Cosmo—in Scotland almost exclusive to the House of Gordon—was introduced to the family in 1720 by Alexander, 2nd Duke of Gordon (1678-1728), on account of his close friendship with Cosimo de Medici, Grand Duke of Tuscany. So, in every subsequent generation of Gordons, there has been at least one Cosmo.

Gordon Castle, the birth-place of the 4th Duke of Gordon
—and incidentally of the Gordon Highlanders—is now a tragic
ruin. Situated in the delightful parish of Bellie in Morayshire, the property came to the Gordons through the marriage
of Alexander Seton, elder son of Elizabeth Gordon, daughter
and heiress of Sir Adam Gordon and wife of Alexander Seton
of that ilk. In 1449, Alexander Seton assumed the name
of Gordon and was created Earl of Huntly. Then called
Bog-o'-Gight, the first castle was built by him, on or near
the site of the later Gordon Castle, the major portion of
which was erected in the grand manner by the 4th Duke.
The original name Bog-o'-Gight, derived from the 14th century chapel of "Geth" which stood near the castle, is never
heard today but curiously enough the name survives in
another Gordon property, Gight in Aberdeenshire, famous
for its associations with the poet Byron whose mother was a
Gordon of Gight.

Alexander Gordon was nine years old when he succeeded
his father as 4th Duke of Gordon and thus acquired the
vast territories of the family. By the age of twenty-four,
he was tall, handsome, cultured, easy-going, fond of sport
and enormously wealthy. He was also possessed of a title
—the highest in the Peerage after the Royal Family—and
consequently was one of the greatest "catches" in Society.
Although one biographer writes "he had no abilities beyond
mediocrity", one might pose the question—did His Grace
really require any?

The scene now moves south from Gordon Castle in Moray
to Wigtonshire where, from the year 1481, the lands of Monreith had been held by the Maxwell family, a younger branch
of the Maxwells of Caerlaverock. In 1748, there was born
to Sir William Maxwell, 3rd Baronet of Monreith, and his
wife Magdalen, daughter of William Blair of that ilk, a
daughter—their second daughter, whom they called Jane.
The birth took place in Hyndford's Close, Edinburgh, where
Magdalen Blair had a flat on the second floor of a "tenement".
The Maxwells were by no means wealthy and Jane's upbring-

ing was frugal. She turned out to be an attractive child, but rather wild and boisterous and her behaviour was often the despair of her parents. Always out for fun—or notoriety— Jane frequently shocked the douce citizens of Edinburgh with her pranks and when one morning she was seen galloping up the High Street on a sow's back—this was the end. She was banished to the country. In her home county, "Jenny of Monreith" was greatly loved and by the time she "came out" she was known as "The Flower of Galloway", and not without good reason. Jane Maxwell was an unusually striking young woman; vivacious, almost to the point of flamboyance, she was clever, indefatigable and ambitious—and she had a way with men. Thus at eighteen, she took Edinburgh by storm and with characteristic determination wooed and won the most eligible man in Scotland—Alexander, 4th Duke of Gordon. The fact that the young Duke already had a love-child, born on 30th July, 1766, was no deterrent to the forceful Jane Maxwell—on the contrary, it appears to have been an incentive.

The last member of the Gordon trio was George, Marquis of Huntly, the elder son of Alexander, 4th Duke of Gordon, and his wife Jane Maxwell. He was born in Edinburgh on 1st February, 1770, and baptised on 2nd March, his sponsors being King George III (1760-1820); his grand-uncle Lord Adam Gordon, Commander-in-Chief of H.M. Forces in Scotland; and his grandmother Catherine, Duchess of Gordon. At seven years old, the Marquis was described as "a lovely boy" having his mother's "fine eyes". His early education was given him by a Swiss tutor in Geneva but he later went to Eton and from there to St. John's College, Cambridge, where he graduated M.A. On leaving Cambridge, the Marquis entered the 35th Foot Regiment as an Ensign. However, his father having raised an independent Company of Highlanders, the Marquis took this body to the 42nd Regiment, The Black Watch, and was given a Captaincy. In June, 1791, the Marquis's Company was reviewed in Edinburgh by his grand-uncle Lord Adam Gordon—it was on this occasion that the celebrated caricaturist Kay made his drawing "Highland Chieftain"—and the following year the Company paraded on the Links at Aberdeen. Tall and handsome like his father, the young Marquis looked extremely well in regimental dress with kilt and plaid—his mother, who was inordinately proud of him, thought so too.

At this point in the story, we move to London where in twenty-four short years, Jane Maxwell, Duchess of Gordon, had accomplished a great deal. London was at her feet. She was the confidant of Royalty, the undisputed leader of society and of fashion, the intimate friend of William Pitt and Horace Walpole and the social centre of the Tory Party. She was the most powerful woman in town. Yes, "Jenny of Monreith" had come a long way from the obscurity of Hyndford's Close in Edinburgh.

In 1791, the young Marquis of Huntly went up to London to visit his mother and to make his first appearance at Court. To the Duchess of Gordon, this was a wonderful opportunity, so, with her flair for the picturesque and the romantic, and with her unerring sense of timing, she had the Marquis present himself in his regimental uniform complete with Black Watch kilt and plaid—a rare picture for the Court of Hanoverian George III. It was barely nine years since the Act proscribing the wearing of Highland Dress had been repealed and as usual the Duchess scored a hit and was quick to follow it up. She sent a pattern of Black Watch tartan to China and ordered a quantity to be woven in silk. With this material, the Duchess had a magnificent gown "built" for herself and caused a tremendous sensation when she wore it at Court in 1792. She featured in a caricature as "The Tartan Belle". Tartan now became the rage in London and as Matthias D'Amour, the Duchess's groom-of-the-chamber records in his *Memoirs*—"Scarcely a respectable female but wore a tartan waist to her gown at least". Jane Maxwell had scored yet another success.

We now return to Gordon Castle in peaceful Morayshire where Alexander, 4th Duke of Gordon, was in the process of raising a Regiment of Fencibles for his Sovereign. On his son's twenty-fourth birthday, the Duke had received from the Secretary of War, the official *Letter of Service* authorising him to raise a Regiment—a fine birthday gift for the young Marquis of Huntly. Of course the Marquis was delighted and so was his mother—to the Duchess it was another opportunity. The muster roll and other details regarding the raising of the Gordon Highlanders are fully set out in J. M. Bulloch's *Territorial Soldiering* (New Spalding Club: 1914) and need not be repeated. However, as the Gordon tartan and the story of the "recruiting kiss" are now of such widespread interest, they demand a word.

Although the Gordons possessed vast territories in the Highlands of Scotland, they were not of Celtic stock. The "de Gourdons" were of Norman extraction having settled in Berwickshire early in the 12th century. In 1319, for loyal services to Robert the Bruce (1306-1329), they obtained a grant of land in Strathbogie, Aberdeenshire, and from that date down the centuries, spread themselves over north-east Scotland until they became one of the most potent forces in the country. The old saying "the Gordons hae the guidin' o't" was no overstatement. Naturally, the House of Gordon —for it was never a Highland clan—had no claim to a tartan but as Alexander, 4th Duke of Gordon, was particularly anxious that his new Highland Regiment should wear a distinctive tartan—a Gordon tartan—he consulted the man who had already supplied him with Black Watch tartan for his son's Company in the 42nd Regiment. This was William Forsyth, Huntly, himself a Black Watch man, and on 15th April, 1793, Forsyth submitted patterns for a new tartan. Three in number, these were based on the Black Watch "sett" with the addition of one, two and three yellow stripes which Forsyth "imagines will appear very lively!". On April 20th, the Duke approved the pattern with the single yellow stripe and the Gordon tartan came into being. Today, one sometimes sees examples of the rejected patterns with two or three yellow stripes of varying thickness—erroneously called "Ancient Gordon" for all three tartans were designed at the same date (1793) and by the same person. Over a century and a half has passed since the Gordon tartan first appeared and today as worn by the famous Regiment, is known the world over. But what of its designer? William Forsyth lies at rest in the quiet kirkyard of Dunbennan in Strathbogie. For the Regimental badge of the Gordon Highlanders, the Duke authorised the use of his own crest *"a buck's head affronte issuing from a crest coronet"* with the motto *"Bydand"*—"Abiding", the whole surrounded by the badge of the Gordon family—the ivy.[9]

We now come to the story of the "recruiting kiss". That the Duchess of Gordon and her five daughters played an important part in recruiting for the Gordon Highlanders there is no doubt. Unfortunately, no contemporary record of their activities has come to light while the first description of the recruiting campaign was written some sixty years after the event. This tells that when campaigning in the various towns and villages, the gay Duchess and her daughters dressed up in Highland bonnets with feathers, tartan scarves, short tartan petticoats with pantaloons. They were usually accompanied by the Duke's piper and offered to dance with any young man willing "to accept the bounty and cockade for King George III and Huntly". Recruits having come forward, a lively reel followed.[10]

At the beginning of the present century, the "recruiting kiss" story first appeared in print. It would seem to have originated in a rumour, circulated by rival recruiters less successful than the Duchess of Gordon and her daughters, that the Lady Madelina Sinclair—one of the daughters—while recruiting for the Gordon Highlanders with her husband Sir Robert Sinclair, "marched through Thurso in the filebeg and hose enlisting men with a kiss and a guinea in her mouth". This rumour was immediately refuted by the Lady Madelina herself. Yet it persisted, as rumours do, and eventually became "attached" to Duchess Jean whose flamboyant character was quite in keeping with the story. Contemporary records make it clear that the guinea was also a rumour, the bounty for recruits being from £20 to £30. The romantic story of the "recruiting kiss" survives. The Marquis of Huntly served with the Gordon Highlanders—

first numbered the 100th Regiment and later the 92nd—for ten years and subsequently became their first Colonel.

With the passing years, the sands began to run out for the Duchess Jean. She had not mellowed with time and had made a great many enemies. Jane Maxwell was still the leader of Society by virtue of her title but she had become brassy and coarse—

> *"The Duchess triumphs in a manly mien;*
> *Loud is her accent and her phrase obscene."*

Eventually, the Duchess became estranged from her husband and her family—she had gone too far. Yet she had done her best for them all. As a match-maker she was without equal and for her daughters had secured three Dukes, one Marquis and a Baronet. Only the Marquis had proved difficult for he suspected insanity in the Gordon family. Duchess Jean, however, set his mind at rest but in so doing staggered society —she declared there was not a drop of Gordon blood in his future wife.

Jane Maxwell, Duchess of Gordon, spent her last years in utter loneliness and misery. On 14th April, 1812, she died in Pulteney's Hotel, Piccadilly, at the age of sixty-three— "more satisfactorily than one could have expected" as her Scots minister succinctly put it. However, to the end Duchess Jean was determined to lead the world of Fashion and, dressed in a fabulous gown of crimson velvet, lay in state for three days. She was carried to the Highlands—to Kinrara near Inverness, her final resting place which she had selected many years before.

Alexander, 4th Duke of Gordon, survived his Duchess, Jane Maxwell, by fifteen years. As already mentioned, the Duke had before his marriage a fine boy whom he called George Gordon. This lad bore a remarkable resemblance to the Duke's legitimate son George, Marquis of Huntly. Hence, in the somewhat unusual circumstances, Duchess Jean had always referred to the boys as "The Duke's George" and "My George". However, during his married life, the Duke had three more children by the same attractive young woman

Jane Christie, whose parents worked on the Duke's estate at Fochabers. Jane had been promised in marriage to a local lad but on hearing of this, the Duke "whisked her off to Gordon Castle in his carriage" in the true Lochinvar tradition. Eight years after the death of Duchess Jean, Alexander, 4th Duke of Gordon, married his lover Jane Christie, the wedding taking place in Bellie Kirk, near Gordon Castle. The parish minister the Rev. William Rennie conducted the ceremony and Jane became Duchess of Gordon. She died in 1824 and lies at rest in Bellie kirkyard in an impressive Ionic temple erected over her tomb by the Duke who died three years later. He was interred at Elgin Cathedral.

George Gordon, Marquis of Huntly, succeeded to the Dukedom on his father's death in 1827. After a somewhat hectic career, the Marquis had married in 1813 Elizabeth Brodie of Arnhall, Kincardineshire, the daughter of an extremely wealthy east India merchant. A quiet, saintly woman, it is said that Elizabeth was "the climax to his rackety life" yet they were very happy. George, 5th Duke of Gordon, died in London on 28th May, 1836, and as a biographer records "he had no issue, legitimate at least".[11] The Dukedom of Gordon, created in 1684, therefore became extinct while the Marquisate of Huntly devolved on the last Duke's kinsman the Earl of Aboyne. A trio of "gey" Gordons had faded from the scene.[12]

Facing. 1. Rev. John Welch, Ayr.
2. Jane Maxwell, Duchess of Gordon.

1

2

1

2

24

GATEWAY TO THE YEARS

"The church and clergy here, no doubt,
Are very much akin;
Both weather-beaten are without,
Both empty are within."

—Jonathan Swift.

LIKE many another ancient Scottish burgh, Aberdeen was at one time noted for its picturesque and historic closes, pends and courts. Such streets as the Shiprow, Castle Street, the Upper and Nether Kirkgates, the Guestrow and the Gallowgate all had their quota of interesting closes few of which survived the great slum clearances of 1920-1930. Nevertheless, unsavoury as a number of these closes undoubtedly were, they did form a definite link with the city's past for most of them were connected with, and indeed frequently bore the names of, families long associated with Aberdeen and whose work and worth had enriched the burgh's heritage.

The entries to several of these closes and courts were features of architectural importance and added a distinctive note to the frontages of the older streets. Perhaps the finest of these still in its original place, is the entry to St. Paul's Episcopal Church at No. 61 Gallowgate—opposite Greyfriars House—and although it is passed by hundred of people every day, few are aware of its significance.

Facing. 1. Gateway, St. Paul's Episcopal Church,
    Gallowgate.

  2. Cot-town of Balgownie.

97

H

This fascinating pend was formerly the only access to "the Episcopal Meeting House" (old St. Paul's Episcopal Chapel) built in 1721, for at that date Loch Street—laid-out in 1840 and from which access to the chapel was subequently obtained—was a mere footpath running round the east side of the then diminishing Loch of Aberdeen. The irregular lines of Loch Street are, of course, due to the asymetrical shore of the loch which it skirted.

Both the gateway to the pend and St. Paul's Episcopal Chapel were the work of a little-known but talented architect Archibald Jaffray, a Quaker, of the Kingswells family. Described as a "handsome and commodious" building, the chapel was eventually demolished and in 1865 was replaced by the present church, now abandoned. The gateway is therefore doubly interesting in that it is the only surviving portion of the original chapel and is the sole example remaining of the work of Archibald Jaffray in the city.

In the 18th century, church-going was much more general than it is today and people travelled greater distances in order to attend their own particular form of worship. Thus contemporary records tell of the long line of carriages, complete with coachmen, postilions and footmen, waiting along the Gallowgate while their owners attended Divine Service in St. Paul's. The Service over, the scene in the chapel court can well be imagined—not a colourful scene, of course, for unlike today, blacks, greys with perhaps a daring touch of purple, were the only acceptable colours for worship. What the scene may have lacked in colour was more than compensated for by the worshippers themselves, many of them highly colourful personalities. Perhaps the most noted of these was Henrietta, Duchess of Gordon, whose elaborate coat of arms was proudly displayed on the "fore-briest" of her private "laft" in the chapel and was preserved in the later church.

Henrietta, Duchess of Gordon, was the only daughter of the celebrated soldier Charles Mordaunt, Earl of Peterborough and Monmouth, by his wife Carey Fraser of Durris—the popular Lady-in-Waiting to Catherine of Braganza, Queen of Charles II (1660-1685). Brilliant and active, Henrietta married Alexander, 2nd Duke of Gordon, and like her husband was an ardent Jacobite. Their third son was Lord Lewis Gordon about whom was written the well-known Jacobite song—*"O send Lewis Gordon hame"*. He attended St. Paul's from infancy until the '45 after which he left Scotland to die in exile. Another youthful worshipper was the poet Lord Byron, then living with his mother in Broad Street.

But many famous people have passed under the dignified old archway of the chapel court in the Gallowgate—John Wesley the preacher; Dr. Samuel Johnson and his companion James Boswell; Francis Peacock the musician and dancing-master immortalised in the name of another pend—Peacock's Close; the Gregory family of Drumoak—kinsmen to the celebrated Rob Roy MacGregor; and many members of well-known county families including the Bannermans of Elsick, the Buchans of Auchmacoy, the Gordons of Haddo and the Inneses of Learney.

Truly the entry to St. Paul's may be called a "gateway to the years" for it has stood for over two centuries unscathed, except for the loss of its remarkably fine wrought-iron spandril so carefully preserved for posterity through two World Wars only to be irreparably damaged through a lorry-driver's carelessness in time of peace. The dignified old archway has seen many changes, old friends and neighbours disappear and new ones arrive. It has witnessed the re-alignment of the historic Gallowgate with all that this implies.

25

BALGOWNIE'S COT-TOWN

*"It is a reverend thing to see an ancient
castle or building not in decay."*

—Francis Bacon.

IN these days of rush and turmoil of life's ever-increasing tempo, it is refreshing to come across some haven where time seems to stand still and where one may reflect on all that has gone before. Such a haven is the Cot-town of Balgownie near the famous bridge immortalised by the poet Byron.

The name Balgownie is derived from the Gaelic *poll gonaidh*—"pool of bewitchment"—that dark, drear, sinister-looking pool on the River Don located immediately west from the picturesque Brig o' Balgownie. Now styled the "Black Nook Pot", it has been the scene of many drowning tragedies.

The ancient ford over the River Don lay to the east of the bridge, just below the aforesaid pool, and the old approach road to the ford from Don Street may still be traced. Of course the advantages of having a bridge over the river at this point must have been obvious for a great many years before any definite scheme for erecting one was formulated, Technical skill and sufficient money were the main problems and it was not until the end of the 13th century that both became available.

Balgownie is first noted in the year 1284 when the name of Malcolm de Pelgoueni, a provost of Aberdeen, appears as an executor to his friend Richard Cementarius—Richard the mason, who himself occupied the civic chair in 1272 and who

was master mason at the building of the Brig o' Balgownie.
Malcolm's lands lay along the north bank of the River Don,
his "fortalice and mensal lands of Pelgoueni" standing high
above the river almost opposite Tillydrone "motte". Malcolm
de Pelgoueni was an immensely wealthy burgess of Aberdeen
and doubtless financed the scheme for building the bridge, at
least in its early stages.

It was initially to the ford—and subsequently to the
bridge—that the Cot-town of Balgownie owes its origin, for
the crossing over the Don at this point became the most
important one on the lower reaches of the river. Then, the
main road north from Aberdeen via Old Aberdeen and the
lands of Seaton, reached the river at "Pelgoueni" and immediately on crossing the Don divided—the right branch leading
to the coast, the left branch to Old Meldrum. It was at this
point of separation that the Cot-town—so-called to distinguish
it from the Sea-town (Seaton), a hamlet on the south bank
of the Don nearer the North Sea—sprang up.

It would seem that the Brig o' Balgownie was in the course
of erection when it attracted the attention of Thomas the
Rhymer whose penchant for predicting doom has earned for
him a special place in Scottish history. Possibly it was when
returning from his visit to the Buchan area—where he excelled
himself in several outbursts of prophetic malediction—that
the Rhymer made his well-known pronouncement against the
bridge:—

> *"Brig o' Balgownie, wicht's thy wa',*
> *Wi' a wife's ae son an' a mare's ae foal*
> *Doon shalt thou fa'."*

That was six hundred years ago—but of course Thomas the
Rhymer was never one to look for speedy results.[13]

Down the centuries, the Brig o' Balgownie has figured in
history. Its familiar Gothic arch is known to thousands who
have never seen it, for its graceful lines, its unique setting
and its romantic associations have made it a mecca for artists
and photographers alike. It is indeed one of Aberdeen's main
tourist attractions as is the Cot-town at its northern end.

Writing of the Cot-town at the beginning of the present century, Ella Hill Burton Roger says—"the red-tiled cottages, of which there used to be many more than there are now, complete a scene dear to the heart of the travelled Aberdonian who comes back from abroad to feast his eyes on it once more. All else is changed to him!   New Aberdeen is unrecognisable; but the Brig o' Balgownie is the same, and indeed after six hundred years looks practically as it did in Bruce's reign".

The oldest cottage in the Cot-town is that nearest the Brig o' Balgownie. It probably dates from around 1600. Originally known as "The Black Nook Alehouse", it long served the needs of weary, thirsty travellers on their way to and from the north. The alehouse stood at the junction of the two north roads already referred to. The coast road has been re-named Bridge Terrace—a somewhat "mealy-mou'd" piece of 20th century urbanity, while the Old Meldrum road —now known as the Black Nook Brae—is but a steep, narrow lane open only to pedestrians until it joins Balgownie Road.

Local records tell that "a good dram could be had in the clean interior" of "The Black Nook Alehouse", yet there was a drawback—at least from the proprietor's point of view. Near the gable-end of the alehouse, a spring gushed from the living rock on which the cottage stands. Clear and invigorating, the "Black Nook Spring" was frequently the means of prejudicing sales. About the year 1871, the spring was piped and still serves as a drinking fountain.

The other dwellings along Bridge Terrace were latterly occupied by lax (salmon) fishers of the nether Don and until comparatively recently were white-washed in the fisher tradition. The two-storied house at the east end of Bridge Terrace is a prominent feature. Built about the year 1730 as an inn, it was known as "The Fore-bank" and until recent years the "tethering-rings" for securing horses were a feature of the entrance doorway.

The recent restoration of the picturesque Cot-town of Balgownie is an excellent illustration of how an old hamlet of sub-standard dwellings can be converted and brought into line with present-day requirements and so enhance and enrich a locality redolent of the past.

26

AUTHOR, EDITOR AND HISTORIAN

*"A prophet is not without honour, save
in his own country, among his own kin,
and in his own house."*
—St. Matthew XI 57.

WHEN walking with a friend in the Dean Cemetery,
Edinburgh, where so many who have contributed
to Scotland's fame lie at rest, we stopped before
a Celtic cross of elaborate design. My friend exclaimed—
"Isn't that the coat of arms of Aberdeen?"—and sure enough
it was, a carefully cut reproduction of the ancient seal as
used in the burgh from the year 1430. What was the
link between Aberdeen and this impressive memorial in an
Edinburgh cemetery?

*   *   *

The story starts in the remote Aberdeenshire parish of
Leochel-Cushnie on Donside where, towards the end of
the 18th century, Christian Leslie (1776-1859) and Joseph
Robertson (1775-1817) were married. Both were natives of
the district and their mortal remains lie in the secluded
kirkyard of Leochel although the headstone marking their
grave would seem to have perished. Fortunately, its inscription was recorded by Andrew Jervise in his *Epitaphs and
Inscriptions*:—

> Joseph Robertson, late merchant in Aberdeen,
> who departed this life 18th February, 1817,
> aged 42, and of Christian Leslie, his spouse,
> who died 11th March, 1859, aged 83 years."

It would appear that as a young man, Joseph Robertson left Leochel-Cushnie to seek employment in London but returned to the north-east shortly before his marriage. Subsequently, he and his wife settled in Aberdeen—at No. 37 Woolmanhill—where he opened a small general merchant's shop. Here his family was born—Joseph and Anne—and here he died in 1817. Left with a son and daughter to support, Christian Robertson continued the Woolmanhill shop until they were of age to earn their own livelihood.

Born on 17th May, 1810, Joseph Robertson was seven years old when his father died. However, despite her limited means, Christian Robertson sent her son to Udny Academy, a small boarding school in Aberdeenshire with a high reputation for scholarship. Under the redoubtable "Bisset of Bourtie", the Rev. James Bisset, D.D. (1794-1872), Moderator of the General Assembly, this rural academy produced many remarkable men, among them Lieut-Col. Sir James Outram, Bt., William Leslie of Warthill, M.P., Professor Samuel Trail, and Sir John Forbes, Bt. of Craigievar.

From Udny Academy, young Joseph Robertson went to Aberdeen Grammar School and from there to Marischal College. He is said to have been an average student, his only distinguishing characteristic being his unusual feats of strength and daring. During his sojourn at the Grammar School and at College, his most intimate friend—and for obvious reasons of mutual interests—was John Hill Burton, later to become Historiographer Royal for Scotland. Both Robertson and Burton entered law offices in Aberdeen, the former that of James Simpson, advocate, a typical legal man of his time, a fine lawyer and possessed of wide literary tastes.

At this stage, Joseph Robertson became actively interested in the "Society of Writers", a literary and debating society formed chiefly of young men of the legal profession in Aberdeen. In this association, Robertson played a leading part, his contributions being characterised by the detailed accuracy of the information given. A keen lover of nature, he spent all his holidays in exploring the wilder parts of Deeside.

By the age of twenty, Joseph Robertson was already show-ing his abilities as a writer, his output at this time being directed chiefly to *The Aberdeen Magazine*, an ambitious venture sponsored by Lewis Smith, a well-known Aberdeen bookseller. Among Robertson's outstanding contributions to this publication were "A Day Among the Hills", "Deeside", and "Logan on the Celts".

Robertson's first book—*A Guide to the Highlands of Deeside*—appeared in 1831, not however under his own name but under the pseudonym "James Brown". The first of its kind to be published in the north-east, the *Guide* was an immediate success and passed through fifteen editions. How-ever, only with the appearance of the twelfth edition in 1869 —after Robertson's death—was the identity of the author revealed, indeed so closely had the secret been kept that Robertson himself wrote the review of his own book!

Nevertheless, as one would expect, Robertson's literary work in Aberdeen brought him little remuneration and in 1833 he moved south to Edinburgh entering the well-known publishing house of Oliver and Boyd. At this time, their *Edinburgh Cabinet Library* was in course of preparation and Robertson threw himself into this work with customary zeal. He also had a hand in the firm's *Edinburgh Almanack*.

As his limited time permitted, he worked on a history of Aberdeen—*The Book of Bon-Accord*—part one appearing in 1839. To all subsequent historians of the city, this remark-able book is of inestimable value and it is ever to be regretted that the second part was never published.

Shortly after the appearance of *The Book of Bon-Accord*, and on his appointment as editor of the weekly Conservative newspaper *The Constitutional*, Robertson returned to Aber-deen, and before the end of 1839, along with his friend John Stuart, advocate, had planned and formed The Spalding Club. This was a fresh outlet for Robertson's unique gifts and energy and many of the Club's early publications were edited by him including *A History of Scots Affairs* (3 Vols.),

Collections for a History of the Shires of Aberdeen and Banff (3 Vols.), and *Passages from the Diary of General Patrick Gordon.*

In 1843, Robertson moved to Glasgow on his appointment as editor of the *Glasgow Constitutional.* He remained there for six years until a similar post was offered him in Edinburgh with *The Courant,* principal newspaper of the Conservative Party in Scotland. Three years later, Joseph Robertson accepted the post he had always felt was his destiny—that of Curator of the Historical Department at H.M. Register House, Edinburgh. Here he made his greatest contribution to Scottish history and for nine years worked literally night and day at the task he loved.

In the spring of 1866, Robertson following a diagnosis that he was suffering from a malignant disease of the throat, realised he had but a short time to live and worked against time until the end came on 13th December, 1866. He was laid to rest in the Dean Cemetery. Robertson was survived by his wife Anne Lanham, two sons, two daughters and his sister Anne who had married William McCombie, farmer and co-founder of the Aberdeen Free Press.

"Save in his own country, among his own kin", Joseph Robertson was widely appreciated and honoured. In 1864, he received the LL.D. from Edinburgh University and on his death Queen Victoria conferred a pension on his widow "for his services to literature generally, and especially in the illustration of the ancient history of Scotland". His friends in the Spalding Club raised the monument over his grave—a fitting tribute to a very remarkable man and designed by his friend the Scottish artist James Drummond, R.S.A. No memorial to Joseph Robertson will be found in his native Aberdeen so the reproduction of the city's ancient seal on the Edinburgh memorial is significant—it is the symbol of the "Bon-Accord" he loved and whose history was so close to his heart.[14]

27

ALL'S WELL THAT ENDS WELL

"Finis coronat opus"—(The end crowns the work).
—Motto of the Hammermen.

DURING the black-out of the Second World War, dignified Golden Square in Aberdeen was the scene of an unfortunate casualty, happily not a human casualty, but one which ended the life of a once-familiar landmark—or so it was thought at the time.

The story actually begins in the year 1222 when Alexander II (1214-1249) granted a charter to Aberdeen wherein he set down various regulations pertaining to craftsmen working within the Royal burgh. This charter may well be regarded as the origin of that institution now known as the Incorporated Trades of Aberdeen.

Seven in number, the Incorporated Trades include the Bakers, Fleshers, Hammermen, Shoemakers, Tailors, Weavers and the Wrights and Coopers. The early history of these trades is lost in the mists of antiquity but by the 15th century there is ample record of their activities. The valuable work by Ebenezer Bain—*A History of the Aberdeen Incorporated Trades*—gives a detailed account of the formation, rules and scope of each of the seven trades.

With the passing centuries, the trades expanded and prospered. They acquired parcels of land both in and outwith the burgh and these they subsequently feued and by this means derived—as indeed they do today—a considerable revenue for their provident and charitable purposes.

One of the most important trades was, and still is, the Hammermen under whose jurisdiction came a number of other trades "using the hammer", but whose numerical strength was relatively small. These other craftsmen became members of the Hammermen trade by what was called "tolerance" and by the year 1686 ten of these trades were included in the Guild of Hammermen. Numbered in this group were the Goldsmiths, a small body of craftsmen, but financially quite powerful and who, down the years, provided a number of officials for the Hammermen trade.

By the end of the 17th century, the Hammermen, like the other trades, had acquired various pieces of land in and around the burgh. Among these were St. John's Croft and Greathead Croft, lying to the south and west of Windmill Brae, and the Longlands which included the ground to the west of Union Terrace Gardens.

With the laying out of Union Street and the building of Union Bridge in the early 1800's, the time became ripe for the Hammermen to develop the lands they held in that area. Thus in 1806, on St. John's Croft and Greathead Croft, they laid-out a new street leading south from Union Street. Appropriately, the Hammermen called this street Crown Street, after the heraldic charge on the "Honour Point" of their armorial bearings—the crown—matriculated at Lyon Court in 1682.

Having completed their Crown Street scheme, the Hammermen proceeded to lay-out another area on the north side of Union Street—on the Longlands which had belonged to the Goldsmiths. Thus today, we find an interesting group of street-names, all deriving from the crown on the Hammermen's armorial bearings and linked with the ancient craft of the Goldsmiths—Golden Square, North and South Silver Street, Diamond Street, Place and Lane, and Ruby Place and Lane.

The scheme for the development of the Longlands was completed about the year 1821 and Golden Square became Aberdeen's most fashionable quarter. One of its major attractions was that it had its own water supply, not in every house, of course, but from a deep, spring well situated on the north side of the Square. It was known as the Hammermen's Well and each householder in the Square had a key to the water pump. Thus, every morning and evening, domestics from the various households in the Square would foregather at the well to draw water for their particular needs. Doubtless these daily meetings provided excellent opportunities for the exchange of gossip.

Eventually, "a key to the Hammermen's Well" became one of the entrance "essays" to the Hammermen trade and occasionally one these fine, hand-made "essay" keys makes its appearance in some saleroom. But what of the Well? With the introduction of piped water from a main supply, the spring water from the Hammermen's Well was eventually cut off and the old pump became "redundant". Despite this, it remained "on guard" for many years, a distinctive feature of Golden Square. However, during the black-out of the Second World War, the pump was accidentally knocked down and badly damaged. In this state it lay derelict until the end of hostilities in 1945 when it was "rescued", carefully repaired and re-erected—in an Aberdeen garden where it stands today, an object of unusual interest to all who see it.

28

SOLVED BY A MEDAL

"I shot an arrow into the air,
It fell to earth, I knew not where."

—Longfellow.

ON the Aberdeen-Ellon road (A92), just beyond the 10th milestone, stands the farm of Cairneylaw. Built into the south gable of its steading is a stone bearing an inscription, a puzzle to many people, for it can be seen from the main road. The stone is obviously an ancient one but this only serves to deepen the mystery for the inscription simply reads—"A CADET".

At first glance, the mystery of the inscription would appear to be well-nigh insoluble but if we go back six centuries the solution can be found and the fascinating story of the inscription told.

In the year 1318, in recognition of his loyal services to Robert the Bruce (1306-1329), one Robert de Skene, received a charter of the lands of Skene in Aberdeenshire, thus establishing the family in north-east Scotland.

With the passing centuries, the Skenes prospered and expanded. Consequently, in the 16th and 17th century records of Aberdeen, Skenes are found occupying a variety of positions in the life of the burgh—provosts, magistrates, ministers, advocates, burgesses and merchants, etc. During this period, one of the most noted burgesses was Robert Skene whose gifts to the city were many. He died in the

110

year 1643 when his fortune passed to his son Alexander, a very remarkable man whose name survives through his unique contribution to Scottish literature. He was author of *Memorialls for the Government of the Royal Burghs in Scotland, A Succinct Survey of the City of Aberdeen* and several other works, all of which are extremely valuable today.

Alexander Skene lived at the time when religious intolerance was at its height and when he, a magistrate of the Royal burgh of Aberdeen, became a Quaker, his colleagues on the burgh council were profoundly shocked. Thereafter, both Skene and his wife Lilias Gillespie—who was Scotland's first poetess—suffered many hardships on account of their religious beliefs. They had a family of ten and it is interesting to note that their eldest son John became Governor of the Quaker State of New Jersey in America.

In 1657, Alexander Skene acquired the lands of Newtyle in the Aberdeenshire parish of Foveran. Whether there was a mansion-house on the Newtyle property when Skene purchased it or whether he built one cannot now be determined for Newtyle House was subsequently demolished and no record of the building would seem to have been preserved. At all events, Skene disposed of Newtyle in the year 1680 reserving certain liferents for himself, his wife and family. He died in 1693 and his wife Lilias Gillespie four years later. In accordance with Quaker tradition, Skene and his wife were not interred in the family vault at St. Nicholas Church, Aberdeen, but in the remote and now almost forgotten Quaker burial ground at Kingswells where they lie in unmarked graves alongside others of their persuasion including Aberdeen's celebrated Quaker provost, Alexander Jaffray of Kingswells.

Now Aberdeen Grammar School possesses a unique collection of Archery Medals—relics of those far off days when skill in any particular sport entitled the winner to give a medal rather than to receive one. In the collection is one presented in 1674 by a schoolboy archer, John Skene of Newtyle, nephew of the above-mentioned Alexander. The medal displays the full armorial bearings of Skene of Newtyle and engraved on the motto ribbon is the clue to the mysterious inscription at Cairneylaw Farm, Foveran.

When the last of the Skene family left Newtyle, their home was eventually demolished and local farmers—with the Aberdeenshire eye to economy—collected and removed the stones from the site for use elsewhere. Among these stones was a fragment bearing part of the Skene of Newtyle motto and this was subsequently built into the steading at Cairneylaw Farm. The fragment, of course, has no meaning until the engraved motto on the Grammar School Archery Medal is read—"SORS MIHI GRATA CADET"—("A pleasant lot shall fall to me"). At Cairneylaw only the last six letters of the motto survive to puzzle posterity—hence "A CADET".

Facing. 1. Woolmanhill, a century ago.
2. The Hammermen's Well.

112

1

2

1

2

3

29

THE GORDONS OF GORDONSTOUN

"Oh! wha hasna heard o' that man o' renown,
The wizard, Sir Robert of Gordonstoun?
The wisest o' warlocks, the Morayshire chiel,
The despot o' Duffus an' frien' o' the De'il!"

THE story of any family may aptly be called a mosaic —"*a work in which the design is formed by many small pieces*". Surveyed over a period of time, every family has its own mosaic—its own particular pattern of life which sometimes becomes obscure. It is then necessary to re-assemble the small pieces so that the pattern may be re-created and appreciated as a design.

An interesting example of a family mosaic is that of the Gordons of Gordonstoun. Although this Morayshire family was neither one of the most noted nor one of the most powerful of our Scottish families, its mosaic forms a fascinating picture and tells an unusually interesting story which covers several centuries.

The founder of the Gordonstoun family was Robert Gordon of Kynmonowie. He was a singularly talented man and a most fortunate one—especially in his choice of ancestors. As these played an important part in the destinies of the Gordon family, some reference to them is appropriate.

Facing.   1. Archery medal of John Skene.

           2. Robert Gordon of Kynmonowie.

           3. Sir Robert Gordon "the Wizard".

113

Robert Gordon of Kynmonowie was the fourth son of Alexander Gordon, 12th Earl of Sutherland, by his wife Lady Jean Gordon, daughter of George, 4th Earl of Huntly. The Huntly Gordon's succession to the Earldom of Sutherland should be explained. In 1492, John, 8th Earl of Sutherland, became insane and died in 1508 leaving a son and a daughter. Unfortunately, the son, who succeeded as John, 9th Earl of Sutherland, suffered from his father's malady and in consequence the succession passed to his sister Elizabeth, Countess of Sutherland. In 1500, Elizabeth had married Adam Gordon of Aboyne, second son of George, 2nd Earl of Huntly, by his second wife the Princess Annabella, daughter of James I (1406-1437). Thus Adam Gordon assumed the courtesy title of Earl of Sutherland and on his wife's death at Aboyne Castle in 1535, their grandson John Gordon succeeded as 11th Earl of Sutherland. He was the grandfather of Robert Gordon of Kynmonowie who, through the Princess Annabella, was descended from the Royal House of Stewart.

The Princess Annabella was one of those Royal ladies of whom history says very little and what is recorded is ineffably sad. The younger sister of James II (1437-1460), the Princess was betrothed in 1444 to Louis, Count of Geneva, and immediately left Scotland to live in her fiancé's country. At this time, intrigue was rife at the Court of France and one day, shortly before her marriage, the unfortunate Annabella found herself redundant. However, the Princess accepted the situation calmly—and the solatium of 25,000 crowns with alacrity. She set sail for Scotland landing at Kirkcudbright in 1448 and the following year was married off to George, 2nd Earl of Huntly. The Princess was Huntly's second wife, the ambitious Earl having divorced his first wife immediately this opportunity to link the "gey" Gordons with Scotland's Royal House presented itself.

By the Princess Annabella, the Earl of Huntly had four sons and four daughters. In 1471, however, the unhappy Princess was divorced and five years later died in complete obscurity. Huntly's third wife was Elizabeth Hay of Erroll who bore him three daughters. Catherine, the eldest of these, appears to have inherited her father's insatiable ambition— or more likely was part of it—for she eventually married the adventurer Perkin Warbeck and so became Duchess of York.

As already mentioned, the mother of Robert Gordon of Kynmonowie was Lady Jean Gordon, daughter of George, 4th Earl of Huntly—"the fat lurdane" who died of a stroke on the battlefield of Corrichie in 1562. The Lady Jean had been previously married to James Hepburn, 4th Earl of Bothwell. She, like the unhappy Princess Annabella, was the victim of an ambitious husband and accordingly, when the ruthless Bothwell saw the chance of linking himself with the Royal House, he divorced her to marry Mary, Queen of Scots. It is curious that Bothwell's unhappy childhood should have been spent near Gordonstoun—at Spynie Palace, the stronghold of his uncle Patrick, Bishop of Moray, and that it was possibly the last place he visited in Scotland when fleeing for his life following the Queen's surrender at Carberry Hill in 1567.

Such is the background story of Robert Gordon of Kynmonowie, founder of the Gordonstoun family, who was born at Dunrobin Castle in Sutherland on 14th May, 1580. His early years were passed in Dornoch where, with his eldest brother John, 13th Earl of Sutherland, he attended the parish school. At the age of sixteen, Robert proceeded to St. Andrew's University and from thence to Edinburgh where he spent three years studying philosophy. In 1602 he went abroad but returned home in 1606—as he himself records— two months after "the detestable powder treason of the fyth of November, 1605 yeirs", when he entered the service of his kinsman James VI (1567-1625). Three years later he was knighted.

In 1613. Sir Robert Gordon of Kynmonowie married Louise Gordon, only daughter and heiress of John Gordon of Glenluce, Dean of Salisbury, and his wife Dame Genewieu Petau, daughter of Gideon Petau, Lord of the Isle of France. By Louise Gordon, Sir Robert had four sons and three daughters all of whom were born in England. Like her husband, Lady Louise was also in the Royal Service being Lady-in-Waiting to the Princess Elizabeth, daughter of James VI and I, who married the Elector-Palatine Frederick V and later became Queen of Bohemia. Curiously enough, it was Princess Elizabeth's descendants in the Hanoverian line who ousted the Stewart descendants of her only surviving brother Charles.

Sir Robert Gordon of Kynmonowie had a long and distinguished career in his country's service. In 1625 he was created a Baronet of Nova Scotia by Charles I (1625-1649)—the premier Baronet of the Order—and was appointed a Privy Councillor for life. Although his family had always resided in England, he determined that eventually they should settle in Scotland and accordingly, in 1638, he purchased two ancient and historic Morayshire properties "benorth the Loch of Spynie"—the Bog of Plewland and Hogstoun. To these he subsequently added Little Drainie, Pethnick, Burnside, Elles and Bellornie, the whole—by a charter under the Great Seal dated 20th June, 1642—being erected into a barony called Gordonstoun. *Circa* 1650, Sir Robert built Gordonstoun House where he died in 1656. Today, Sir Robert Gordon of Gordonstoun, is best known as a historian for his *Genealogical History of the Earldom of Sutherland* is one of the most valuable Scottish documents extant. Sir Robert was succeeded by his son Sir Ludovick Gordon, 2nd Baronet of Gordonstoun. Sir Robert's daughter Katherine become the wife of Colonel David Barclay of Ury in Kincardineshire, a member of the old Aberdeenshire family of Towie-Barclay of whom Prince Barclay de Tolly—the "father of the Russian Army"—was one of the most distinguished (see Chapter 19). Katherine and David Barclay were the parents of Robert Barclay the "Apologist for the Quakers". Sir Robert Gordon's younger son, Robert, purchased the lands of Cluny in Aberdeenshire. He was the father of Robert Gordon described in the Jacobite Lists as "younger of Cluny, Advocate".

Sir Ludovick Gordon, 2nd Baronet of Gordonstoun, has been called "The Improver" for he spent much of his time enhancing Gordonstoun House and its policies. Sir Ludovick married Elizabeth, daughter of Sir Robert Farquhar of Mounie in Aberdeenshire who brought the property of Ryehill in the Garioch to the Gordonstoun family. During Sir Ludovick's lairdship, the Gordonstoun household appears to have been unusually large for, in addition to his own children—six in number—his sister Katherine Barclay and her family resided there until her death in 1663. Thus at Gordonstoun were two young Roberts—cousins—Robert Gordon, later to be known as "The Wizard Laird" of Gordonstoun, and Robert Barclay, the Quaker.

In 1686, Sir Ludovick died and was succeeded by his son Sir Robert Gordon, 3rd Baronet of Gordonstoun. As a young man, Sir Robert travelled extensively, studied at various continental universities and eventually became one of the most accomplished men of his time. A close friend of his kinsman James VII and II (1685-1689), Sir Robert and his cousin Robert Barclay the Quaker were frequently at Court and indeed were among the last to see the king at Whitehall before he went into exile. Sir Robert was a keen business man and in 1664 was admitted a Burgess of Aberdeen.

At Gordonstoun House, Sir Robert assembled a remarkably fine library and chemistry being his special interest, fitted up a laboratory for his own use. However, his unusual accomplishments soon became suspect in the Morayshire area and he was credited with being in league with the Devil.

> *"The man whom the folks o' auld Morayshire feared,*
> *The man whom the frien's o' auld Satan revered,*
> *Oh! never to mortal was evil renown*
> *Like that o' Sir Robert of Gordonstoun!"*

Thus the most fantastic tales built up around "The Wizard Laird"—and if proof were required there was the terrible gale of 1694 when the nearby barony of Culbin was completely obliterated overnight by the most alarming sand-storm in the country's history. Truly the "Wizard's work". Sir

Robert Gordon was indeed a most remarkable man—his only "crime" being that he was born fully two centuries ahead of his time.

Sir Robert was twice married—to Margaret Forbes, daughter of William, 12th Lord Forbes, and to Elizabeth, daughter of Sir William Dunbar of Hempriggs. By his first wife, he had a daughter Jean who married John Forbes of Culloden, elder brother of Duncan Forbes, Lord President of the Court of Session, remembered for the part he played during and after the Jacobite Rising of 1745. By his second wife, Sir Robert had a family of five, his elder daughter marrying Francis Fraser of Pitmurchie, Torphins. Sir Robert Gordon died in 1704 and was succeeded by his son Robert.

From what information survives, it is Sir Robert Gordon, 4th Baronet of Gordonstoun, who should have been called "The Wizard" for he appears to have been a cruel and vindictive man who exercised his full powers as baron of the barony with relentless fury. "Ill Sir Robert" was twice married—and hated both his wives. His first was Rebecca, eldest daughter of Archibald Dunbar of Thunderton, Elgin. Known in history as "The Lady Arradoul", Rebecca Dunbar was a zealous Jacobite. It was she, who in 1746, nursed Prince Charles through his illness when he lodged at Thunderton House before proceeding to tragic Culloden Moor—and it was in accordance with Rebecca's wish that she was buried in the sheets used by the ill-fated Prince.

"Ill Sir Robert's" second wife was Agnes, daughter of Sir William Maxwell of Calderwood, who bore him four sons and a daughter. Sir Robert detested his second wife quite as much as he hated his first, for, while Rebecca had been an avid and tiresome Jacobite, Agnes was an incurable eccentric. He had heard of the old Scottish superstition that to build a dovecote might hasten a wife's death—so the crafty Baronet built four. However, his plan miscarried for the Lady Agnes survived him for over thirty years. She died in 1808 at Lossiemouth—in a small house surrounded by a very high wall crowned with broken glass to protect her from possible French invasion.

During the Jacobite Rising of 1745, the Jacobite Army—knowing of Sir Robert's Hanoverian sympathies—fell upon Gordonstoun House, carried off the laird a prisoner to Elgin, turned his lady and their family out, shot his pigeons, stole his pork, hams and dried fish and commandeered his three best horses—for the use of Prince Charles himself. All was not lost, however, for the cunning Baronet was quick enough to save his work-horses by concealing them in the caves at Covesea still known as "Sir Robert's Stables".

In 1767, on the death of William, 17th Earl of Sutherland, Sir Robert Gordon laid claim to the Earldom through his great grandfather Sir Robert Gordon, 1st Baronet of Gordonstoun, fourth son of the 12th Earl. However, the claim was decided in favour of Elizabeth, younger daughter of the 17th Earl of Sutherland, who became Countess. She married George Leveson-Gower carrying the Earldom of Sutherland to that family.

Sir Robert Gordon, 4th Baronet of Gordonstoun, died in 1772 and was succeeded by his son Robert. A bachelor, Sir Robert the 5th Baronet, died in 1776 and was succeeded by his brother Sir William, 6th Baronet of Gordonstoun. Sir William was also unmarried and by his death in Edinburgh in 1795, the direct male line of Gordonstoun terminated. The Baronetcy of Gordonstoun then devolved on the Gordons of Letterfourie in Banffshire, while the Gordonstoun Estates passed to the Gordon-Cummings of Altyre.

Such is the family mosaic of the Gordons of Gordonstoun. Their mortal remains lie in the family vault at Michael Kirk, built in 1705 by the Lady Elizabeth, widow of "The Wizard Laird", while their lands have passed into other hands. Already a new pattern is being worked out at Gordonstoun —perhaps some fragments from the old mosaic may find their place in the new setting—who can tell?

30

THE BARON'S GRANARY

"Stone walls do not a prison make
Nor iron bars a cage."

—Richard Lovelace.

STONEHAVEN'S old tolbooth is one of the most attractive and interesting buildings in the county of Kincardine. Situated at the extreme north-east corner of the parish of Dunnottar, overlooking the picturesque little harbour, its fascinating history is closely linked with that of the Keith family.

Towards the end of the 14th century, Sir William Keith, Great Marischal of Scotland, acquired the barony of Dunnottar in the Mearns. He immediately erected for himself a powerful keep-tower on the massive, isolated rock two miles south from Stonehaven—the same rock on which St. Ninian the Apostle of Scotland, had established his church in the 5th century—and here Sir William's descendants lived for upwards of three hundred years. Today, the ruin of their sea-girt stronghold, Dunnottar Castle, is surely one of the most impressive in Scotland. In 1457, King James II (1437-1460) created Sir William's grandson and heir, 1st Earl Marischal.

In addition to the barony of Dunnottar, the Keiths held considerable property in north-east Scotland and among their other estates was that of Inverugie at Peterhead. Thus the early rise to prominence of the two north-east ports—Stonehaven and Peterhead—was largely due to the foresight and

120

influence of the Keiths, Earls Marischal. The parallel which exists in the histories of the two townships is quite marked.

As barons of the barony of Dunnottar, the Earls Marischal, in accordance with the practice of the time, collected most of their rentals "in kind". This had to be collected at some point in the barony convenient to all concerned and, as Keith's stronghold at Dunnottar was out of the question, a site near the harbour of the baron's burgh "Stane-hyve" was selected. Hence the building, now called the tolbooth, but originally styled "the Marischal's granary and store-house", was built on the "northe bulwarke at Stane-hyve".

Curiously enough, a similar building serving the same purpose and having the same name, was erected by the Keiths on the north-east side of Brook Lane, Peterhead. It was demolished about a century ago.

The Stonehaven tolbooth appears to have been built towards the end of the 16th century by William Keith, 4th Earl Marischal—known in history as "William of the Tower". The reason for building the tolbooth has already been given— it was intended to be used as the barony's granary and store-house—and this structure still stands.

In the year 1600, however, and doubtless through the influence of George Keith, 5th Earl Marischal—the founder of Marischal College, Aberdeen—an Act of Parliament was obtained transferring the seat of justice from Kincardine in the parish of Fordoun, the ancient capital of the Mearns "quhair there is neither ane tolbuith nor any house to pairties to lodge", to his own barony "burgh of Stane-hyve" and that it should remain there "in all tym heirefter". This Act, which was of major importance to the county, was confirmed in 1607.

It thus became necessary for the Earl Marischal to provide a suitable and convenient tolbooth for the new county-town so he simply added a wing to his grandfather's granary and store-house on the quay-side. This addition still stands at right angles to the original building at its north-west corner. A "fore-stair" gives access to the tolbooth's cells and the windows of these, complete with their iron grilles, are still to be seen.

This convenient and economical arrangement of tolbooth *cum* granary and store-house continued for many years until the Crown's forfeiture of the Keith estates following the Jacobite Rising of 1745. The tolbooth continued to be used as a prison until around 1767.

Two incidents may be referred to in connection with the tolbooth's history. In 1645, during "The Troubles", Stonehaven and its tolbooth figured when they were "fired" by the Marquis of Montrose and his party. It is recorded that the Earl Marischal, powerless to stop the damage, shut himself up in Dunnottar Castle where he watched "the reek" rising from his burning township.

It would seem that Stonehaven took some time to recover from the attentions of Montrose for eleven years later there comes a brief but unflattering description of the burgh by Captain Richard Franck, sometime Trooper in Cromwell's Army—"a small harbour which they call Steen-hive, but I take the liberty to call it Stinking-hive because it is so unsavoury; which serves only for pirates and picaroons".

In both the Jacobite Risings of 1715 and 1745, Stonehaven's tolbooth featured and it is probably due to the part it played after the '45 that it has become known to thousands of people who have never seen the actual building. For their Jacobite sympathies, a number of Episcopalian ministers were imprisoned in Stonehaven's tolbooth during the winter of 1748-49. Their chapels had been burnt by the Duke of Cumberland's troops but their congregations, nothing daunted, went to the tolbooth where their imprisoned ministers read the Liturgy to them through the gratings of the windows. On occasions, even baptisms were conducted in the same way and the well-known painting by S. W. Brownlow (1868) depicts such a sacrament taking place from the north-east window of the tolbooth. An interesting point in Brownlow's picture should be mentioned. All the artist's "models" were local fisherfolk, the descendants of those who gathered round the tolbooth a century ago. They bore such names as Masson, Leiper, Main, Christie and Johnston—all of them well-known names in the great north-east fishing industry today.

Since 1767, the tolbooth and granary has served many purposes and its history comes down to our own day. A wartime mine, washed into Stonehaven's harbour from the North Sea, exploded and seriously damaged the roof, while the great gale of January, 1953, worked further havoc. However, stoutly built of sandstone, the interesting old structure weathered the passage of time and eventually an appeal for its preservation was launched by the burgh council. This was successful and on 11th September, 1963, the restored building was opened by Her Majesty Queen Elizabeth, The Queen Mother. It is a picturesque reminder of the burgh's romantic past.

31

SIGNS, SYMBOLS AND SUPERMARKETS

"God made the wicked Grocer,
For a mystery and a sign,
That man might shun the awful shop
And go to inns to dine."

—G. K. Chesterton.

TODAY, when almost anything can be bought in super-markets and where customers move about from counter to counter filling wire baskets with the necessities of life, it seems obvious that "the butcher, the baker and the candlestick maker" are on the way out. The emphasis is on speed and impersonal service.

Life was much more tranquil in bygone times and the well-known proverb—"Every man to his trade"—had some point. Nowadays, it is generally in the side streets that we find the old-time trader, the weathered trade-sign still displayed over the doorway of his shop as it has been for two, or perhaps three generations. In Aberdeen few firms ever survive to the fourth. Unlike the present, when projecting signs are so numerous as to cancel out the effectiveness of each other, the trade-signs of the past were relatively few but had real significance, and a number of them may still be seen throughout the city.

The most common of the old trade-signs is, of course, the barbers' pole. It is a reminder of the days when barbers were also chirurgeons and leechers and practised blood-letting. Blood pressure appears to have been just as common in the time of our ancestors as it is today—only they went to the barber instead of to the doctor. When receiving treatment, the "patient" was given a white, cloth-covered pole to grasp. This helped the blood to flow more freely and as the pole frequently become stained with blood, it was accepted by the barbers as their trade-sign. Sometimes, a gold-painted basin was hung from the pole when blood-letting was discontinued by barbers, only the red-and-white pole survived to remind us of their former "trade". The barbers' pole and their "colours"—red and white—are still used by the trade in a variety of forms.

The three brass balls of the pawnbroker is another familiar sign in Aberdeen, appropriately so, for St. Nicholas the city's patron, is also the patron of pawnbrokers. This ancient trade-sign has its origin in the coinage of Bezantium, the golden bezant, which was later adopted by the Lombardy bankers as their emblem. Bezants were introduced to the west by the Crusaders and eventually "three bezants" became the trade-sign of pawnbrokers. Today, many companies associated with finance incorporate bezants on their heraldic bearings a notable example being the Bank of Scotland.

Nowadays, most public-houses have their trade-sign but these are generally the symbol or trademark of some well-known brewing firm. The original trade-sign for a public-house was a simple affair—an evergreen bush—a custom going back to Roman times and associated with the worship of Bacchus, the God of wine. During the middle ages, the practice of hanging evergreen bushes over the door-way of taverns and wine-shops was general but the custom eventually died out. The well-known expression "Good wine needs no bush" derives from the practice.

Perhaps the most familiar and colourful trade-sign to be seen in our streets is the Royal arms "By Appointment". It is also the most exclusive—the sole right of Royal Warrant Holders. The custom of displaying armorial bearings on shops goes back to feudal times when the Sovereign, his family, and the nobility, bestowed their patronage on certain tradesmen. These tradesmen were "By Appointment", permitted to display their patron's arms thereby indicating to the public the excellence of their wares and service. Of course, should the goods ever fall below standard or the tradesman displease his patron, the privilege of displaying the arms was immediately withdrawn. Today, only the Sovereign and certain members of the Royal family bestow patronage on tradesman "By Appointment".

One of the oldest trade-signs in the city—for the provost-ship of Aberdeen must surely be regarded as a "trade"—is the provost's lamps. The practice of placing lamps at the front door of a burgh's senior magistrate originated in England centuries ago when it was the custom to honour him by erecting decorative wooden posts at his door—and these were often used for displaying "official" notices. As time passed, posts were superseded by lamp-standards, the custom being introduced to Aberdeen in 1838.

Less than a century ago, most Aberdeen traders had their signs and a number of these have survived to our own time. Several of the trade-signs are real museum pieces and it is to be hoped they will be preserved for posterity. They form an interesting link between the old-time traders and the modern supermarkets.

32

DEAN'S LODGING

"Houses have distinct personalities either bequeathed to them by their builders or tenants, absorbed from their materials, or emanating from the general environment."

—William Beebe.

A T the south end of the Brig o' Balgownie there stands a charming group of buildings of varying dates. The oldest of these is the so-called Chapter House—rather a misleading name for the building was never church property.

Built on the familiar L-plan, it is obvious that the site of the Chapter House had been most carefully selected, for the house stands high above the River Don and between it and Don Street where that thoroughfare descends rather steeply to Balgownie's picturesque bridge.

The small garden of this delightful house is set in the re-entrant angle of the "L" which faces south-west to trap the sun, and when the house was built, it had commanded an extensive view across the lands of Seaton. Today, of course, grand old trees surround the house and overhang the steep, rocky gorge through which flows the sombre, sinister, slow-moving Don. From the garden, a short flight of rough-hewn steps leads down the rocky bank to a small jetty on the river—tidal at this point—giving access to the North Sea less than a mile eastwards. This maritime access must have been a valuable asset to the property when its merchant owners were engaged in trading with the continent.

The Chapter House has an interesting history. It was built in 1655 by George Cruickshank of Berryhill in the parish of Old Machar, and his wife Barbara Hervie of the Elrick family. George Cruickshank was a prosperous merchant in Aberdeen and a man of substance. He was one of those who received a Warrant from General Monk in 1659 to elect a Commissioner and thereafter Cruickshank's name frequently figures in local affairs. In 1644, he was elected Dean of Guild of Aberdeen.

By his wife Barbara Hervie, George Cruickshank had two sons, George and William. Both were born in the Chapter House but in a record dated 1669 it is stated that "Barbara Hervie, spouse to George Cruickshank, at Bridge of Don, died in child-bed".

Like his father before him, George Cruickshank Yr. was a prosperous merchant in Aberdeen. A magistrate and "Maister of the Kirk and Brig Wark", he married Ann Gordon, a daughter of Alexander Gordon, Provost of Aberdeen in 1688-89. George, the younger, was by far the most colourful member of the family. A perfervid Jacobite, he was "out" in the Rising of 1715, acting as tax-collector for the cause in Aberdeen. He survived the Rising and died in 1737. He might well be called the "father of the catering trade" in the burgh for in 1700 he was granted permission by the Town Council to "set up a coffee-house for the sale of coffee, tea and chocolate". By way of encouragement in the project, the Council waived all his taxes for a period of nineteen years—undoubted proof of the adage "the good old days".

The younger son William—who married Isobel Phanes, daughter of William Phanes, Convener of the Aberden Incorporated Trades—became Provost of Aberdeen in 1728-29 and it is interesting to note it was during his term of office that Robert Gordon made application for the feu in Schoolhill on

1

2

1

2

which his Hospital—later called Robert Gordon's College—was subsequently built.

During the three hundred years of its existence, the Chapter House has seen many changes. In the mid 19th century, it served as a Dame School and it was here that the infant Robert Laws (1851-1934)—later to be known as Laws of Livingstonia, the celebrated missionary, had his first lessons. By this time, the property had been merged in the Seaton Estate which in 1947 was acquired by the Corporation of Aberdeen.

Quite withdrawn from the busy city with which its early merchant owners were so closely associated, the fascinating old Chapter House is truly redolent of other days.

Facing. 1. The Chapter House, Balgownie.

2. Our Ladye's Pity Vault, East and North
St. Nicholas Church.

K

33

ARCHITECTURAL HERITAGE

"He builded better than he knew:
The conscious stone to beauty grew."
—Emerson.

ABERDEEN and "The Granite City" have long been synonymous. This is perhaps unfortunate for it infers that "The Granite City" was the beginning—and some suggest the end—of our building heritage. In actual fact, out of an architectural history extending back more than eight centuries, "The Granite City" era covers only a very brief period.

The earliest mason work extant in Aberdeen dates from the middle of the 12th century. This is the Norman work in the Church of St. Nicholas (the "Toun's Kirk") at the north-west crossing below the spire. It is carried out in dark red sandstone and is easily traceable.

The only other work of this period in the city is a solitary fragment preserved in the Cathedral of St. Machar and serves to remind us of Bishop Matthew Kyninmund's Norman building begun in 1164 and subsequently demolished. The fragment is part of an abacus of a square pier showing the familiar "dog-tooth" ornament of the period. It is of yellow sandstone similar to that used in the building of King William the Lion's "palace" (1181), a small portion of which survives *in situ* below road-level in Trinity Street.

These early works in sandstone raise an interesting point in the story of our building traditions. Although granite

130

has been used from earliest times for rubble walling—usually of surface gatherings—every mediaeval *cementarius* (master-mason) was a craftsman only in sandstone, shaping and cutting this material in the exercise of his craft. They avoided granite for dressed work. The sandstone then used in Aberdeen was quarried at a few places in the county, Kildrummy being the principal source of supply although considerable quantities were shipped to Aberdeen from Covesea in Morayshire. Dressed stones from both these sources—dark red from Kildrummy and yellow from Covesea—may be seen in most of the city's mediaeval buildings and other works.

The next structure of importance to be erected was the famous Brig o' Balgownie, initially the work of Richard Cementarius—Richard the mason. He is the first recorded Provost of Aberdeen, having held office in 1272. Richard, who was the King's master-mason, is known to have been responsible for building the great Tower of Drum and he was also mason for part of Aberdeen Castle on the Castlehill. He died about the year 1294, having founded in 1277 an altar to St. John the Evangelist (patron of the mason craft and also of the wrights). The object of Richard's foundation was for the repose of his soul and that of Elene his wife. For the upkeep of this foundation, he granted various annual rentals to the value of 10/8d. Scots, including one from St. John's Croft—the land now covered by the General Post Office in Crown Street.

In both the Church of St. Nicholas (Collison's Aisle) and the Cathedral of St. Machar (at the central crossing) may be seen some fine examples of work in the Transitional and Decorated Gothic styles. Executed in sandstone *circa* 1370, these works carry us forward to that remarkable era in Aberdeen's architectural history known as "The Granite Interregnum". This period, which occurred between the years 1420 and 1440, has never been satisfactorily explained. At all events, the supply of sandstone appears to have suddenly stopped and granite became the only building material available in the burgh. Under the dynamic direction of Bishop Henry de Lichtoun, a new west front was planned for the Cathedral of St. Machar and it would appear that building operations began soon after the year 1424.

Obviously, the master-mason selected by Lichtoun was more accustomed to castle-building than to church work. He was no accomplished ecclesiastical craftsman, but he certainly knew how to handle granite and on the Cathedral's west front he raised two strongly buttressed fortress-towers, boldly machicolated, for use in times of stress. His seven tall, round-headed windows in the Norman tradition and the great west door—a Doric version of the elaborate doorway of Elgin Cathedral—are unique in this country.

Also erected during "The Granite Interregnum" was St. Mary's Chapel—"Our Ladye's Pity Vault"—that beautiful sanctuary below the East and North Church of St. Nicholas. It was built before the year 1437 by the Lady Elizabeth Gordon "heir of Huntly and Strathbogie" who was buried there in 1438.

Although St. Mary's Chapel is built entirely of granite by an unknown master-mason, it is clear that his knowledge of Gothic forms was far in advance of that possessed by Bishop Lychtoun's mason at the Cathedral. It is interesting to note that in the "Pity Vault" lie the mortal remains of Sir John Gordon, beheaded in the Castlegate in 1562 following the battle of Corrichie.

"The Granite Interregnum" ended about the year 1440 and in the last quarter of that century, a new choir was built at the Church of St. Nicholas. It was carried out in the late Gothic style, the work being executed in sandstone "be measones of the luge"—"Richard Ancram, Andro Murray, James of Barry, Johnne Russell, Matho Wrycht and Johne of Kildrummy"—under the direction of "Johne Gray, maister-measone". Gray does not appear to have been overpaid for his work—"twentie poundis and five merks Scots", per annum, roughly about £1 : 18/11½ Stg. The choir was the citizens's pride and joy but unhappily it was demolished in 1835—on the advice of Archibald Simpson.

Today, the only external feature remaining of the ancient "Toun's Kirk" is the north transept (Collison's Aisle)—"ye gavill of ye croce kirk" with its "faire windo"—seen to advantage from Schoolhill. Here also is St. Michael's doorway built up in 1519 when the window was inserted, and the lead-traceried eaves-apron, unique in Scotland. Unfortunately, this interesting gable is rapidly falling into disrepair and soon will be beyond preservation. The ancient memorials to the city's provosts within the Aisle are also in a shocking state of decay.

The other great building which followed "The Granite Interregnum" is King's College Chapel, begun in 1500. Externally, the chapel's greatest glory is its crown-steeple, one of the two ancient examples left in Scotland. The original crown-steeple was blown down in February, 1633, the present one—the work of George Thomson, master-mason—being erected shortly after. So much has been written about King's College Chapel that repetition is unnecessary.

Another important building in the post "Granite Interregnum" period was Greyfriars' Church, built in 1530. This fascinating building was demolished in 1901 and only its "gryt gavill windo" survives—built into the east end of the present church. Also of this period is the Bridge of Dee, a truly remarkable achievement. Built between the years 1520 and 1527, its master-mason was Thomas Franche, the son of John Franche. Both father and son were King's master-masons.

Alongside Thomas Franche, mention must be made of John Fendour, "vrycht" (wright), who did so much to beautify our mediaeval buildings with his fine "tymmir warke"—among others, the Church of St. Nicholas, St. Mary's Chapel, King's College Chapel and the Cathedral of St. Machar.

The master-masons were, of course, the architects of the time. Their "Luges" appear to have originated in Scotland *circa* 1190, during the reign of William the Lion, and were very close fraternities. A few of the masons who worked in Aberdeen were local men resident in the burgh, but up to the middle of the 16th century, the majority were peripatetic masons, moving about the country wherever their services were in demand. Accordingly, we find the same master-mason—or team of masons—working in various towns and where records are scant or lacking, the masons' marks incised on their dressed stone-work are certain proof of their spheres of activity.

However, by the end of the 16th century, local masons came into their own for the Reformation (1560) brought in its wake a building boom. The transference of considerable wealth from the church to seculars occasioned much activity, particularly in house-building, and this continued until the end of the 17th century.

The mediaeval burgh of Aberdeen was a compact community, its main streets being the Green, the Shiprow, the Castlegate, the Guestrow, the Upper and Nether Kirkgates and the Gallowgate. The buildings lining these streets were originally of timber construction, the first stone-built house in the burgh being erected *circa* 1535. This was the celebrated "stane hoose" of Provost Thomas Menzies which stood on the south side of the Castlegate just west of Marischal Street—on the site now covered by the Bank of Scotland. It was here that the Provost entertained King James V when he visited Aberdeen in 1537 (see Chapter 15).

Gradually, over the years, stone-built houses began to replace the ancient timber ones and it is interesting to note that two of these wooden buildings survived in the Gallowgate until as recently as 1840. It was not until 1731 that the erection of timber-built houses was prohibited within the burgh—a regulation which remained until after the Second World War.

In all the above-mentioned streets, wealthy merchants, burgesses and lairds from the neighbouring counties eventually built their houses, many of them self-contained, but the majority "flatted" and housing several families. In old charters, these are generally referred to as "tenements" or "lodgings". Most of the houses were reached by pends, closes or courts which invariably took their names from the owners—Brebner's Court, Drum's Lane and Sinclair's Close to mention but a few.

Traders soon followed the trend and such places as Candlemaker's Court and Sugarhouse Lane came into being. Of all this precious patrimony, only three notable houses survive —Provost Ross's House in the Shiprow, built in 1593 by Andrew Jamesone, master-mason, father of the celebrated artist George Jamesone; Nos. 24-26 Upperkirkgate, built in 1694; and Provost Skene's House—of the Guestrow group— built in 1545, 1570 and 1670, the 17th century portion being probably the work of John Montgomerie, "meason of Old Rayne", best known for his unusually fine Market Cross in the Castlegate.

In all these houses—and of course, in the Market Cross (1688) and the Tolbooth (1627)—sandstone was used for the dressed work, but the winds of change were blowing. Granite was on the way in as a building material—not quarried granite as we know it today, but surface gatherings, squared and dressed, and it is to the variety in colour of these surface gatherings that our 18th century buildings owe so much of their charm.

The last of the great sandstone buildings was the West Church of St. Nicholas designed by the celebrated architect James Gibbs and built in 1751-55 by James Wyllie, master-mason, of Edinburgh. The collaboration of architect and master-mason is significant.

The 18th century brought Aberdeen's first taste of expansion, and development took place in two areas. Firstly, a new road was envisaged giving direct access from the burgh centre to the harbour—Marischal Street, and secondly, a new residential area was planned on the western outskirts of the town overlooking the picturesque valley of the Denburn— Schoolhill and Belmont Street. Thus, in both these districts buildings of this period may be seen—granite buildings in the new tradition. These include No. 61 Schoolhill (*circa* 1770); the central block of Robert Gordon's College (1731); some

houses in Belmont Street, notably No. 37, erected *circa* 1778;
two fine houses in the Castlegate, Nos. 51-57, built in 1763,
and No. 17 *circa* 1760.

In Queen Street, laid out in 1773, were some unusually
fine examples but these were demolished in 1969-70. The
fascinating gateway to old St. Paul's Episcopal Church also
belongs to this period. Built in 1720, it is the only known
extant work by Archibald Jaffray, architect (see Chapter 24).
In Mackie Place, that little-known, old world corner off Skene
Street is a charming group of houses built towards the end of
the 18th century, while in Marischal Street, laid out in 1768,
are some fine houses which, along with the Chanonry manses
in Old Aberdeen, are the first houses of quarried granite to be
built in the city.

The Marischal Street group—Nos. 42 to 48—are the work
of William ("Sink'em") Smith, the father of John Smith,
architect, who along with Archibald Simpson, was responsible
for the creation of "The Granite City".

The 18th century saw sandstone pass from favour for
building purposes and granite come into general use. As
already mentioned, Aberdeen's first granite buildings were of
surface gatherings, squared and dressed, most of the stone
coming from the Loanhead district of the town where a quarry
of that name was opened about the year 1730. Of Loanhead
granite are Robert Gordon's College (central block) built in
1731 by William Adam of Maryburgh; Nos. 51-57 Castle
Street, built in 1763; and Gilcomston Chapel of Ease (Gilcomston St. Colm's Church), built in 1771 by William Smith—
originally erected for the spiritual well-being of the Loanhead
quarry workers. Although the output from the Loanhead
Quarry was limited, it served the burgh's needs for a number
of years.

About this time, an outcrop of granite on the lands of
Rubislaw was being investigated for the magistrates of Aberdeen with a view to building the new West Church of St.
Nicholas in local stone. This investigation proved negative
and as noted before, the "Toun's Kirk" was built of sandstone
from Craigleith Quarry, Edinburgh.

In 1788, however, the magistrates had before them another report on the "Quarry in the Den of Rubislaw". It stated "the stone is of poor quality, and of no use for building". Accepting this finding, the magistrates thereafter disposed of Rubislaw Quarry for the sum of £160 Scots—roughly about £13 : 6/8d. Stg. Of course history has proved that expert opinion may sometimes be very wide of the mark and it was not until John Gibb, engineer and quarry-master, took over Rubislaw in the early part of the 19th century, that its real value became known. Today it is one of the largest granite quarries in the world.

As the demand for granite increased, other quarries were opened in the north-east, notably Cairngall, Clinterty, Corrennie, Dancing Cairns, Hill o' Fare, Kemnay, Peterhead, Tillyfourie and Tyrebagger. All these contributed towards the building of "The Granite City".

Coinciding with the change-over from sandstone to granite, came a change of designation—from "master-mason" to "architect". Generally speaking, the "master-mason" became the operative builder, while design became the prerogative of the architect. Of course there were neither schools of architecture nor any regular courses on building construction at this time, so it was customary for the embryo architect to serve an apprenticeship with a builder and to study design from the few books available. Had he the means to travel abroad and study the Classic forms from the originals—or if he was fortunate enough to be "adopted" by a wealthy patron—so much the better. Thus in the early days of architectural practice in Aberdeen, recruitment was small and was usually drawn from the dilettante offspring of county gentlemen, or from the sons of wealthy burgesses, merchants or builders.

Among the early Aberdeen architects whose names have been preserved are William Dauney, the maternal uncle of Archibald Simpson; the celebrated James Gibbs, son of a local mason, and who had the good fortune to be "adopted" by the Earl of Mar and in consequence was able to study on the Continent; Archibald Jaffray, scion of the Kingswells family; George Jaffray, the designer of Old Aberdeen's Town House; William Law, who gave us the well-proportioned bridge spanning Virginia Street; James Massie, designer of St. Peter's Roman Catholic Church; and William ("Sink'em") Smith, the "father" of a long line of distinguished Aberdeen architects.

By the end of the 18th century, further expansion of the burgh became an urgent necessity. Extension had been first mooted in 1796 but in 1799 definite steps were taken towards this end. Consequently, on 4th April, 1800, an Act of Parliament authorising the "making of two new streets in the City of Aberdeen" became law and the following year a beginning was made to the formation of what was to become Union Street and King Street.

The building of Union Street—so called in commemoration of the Union of Great Britain with Ireland on 1st January, 1801—has frequently been described. Even by present-day standards it is a remarkable achievement for the obstacles were enormous.

The hub of Aberdeen's first major development scheme was, of course, the Castlegate which had been the city centre for over six centuries. Consequently, it was here that a start was made in the creation of what eventually was to be known as "The Granite City".

The first of the new buildings to be erected in the Castlegate was the Aberdeen Banking Company's office. Built in Castle Street at the North-west corner of Marischal Street— the year 1801, it was designed by James Burn, architect, of Haddington, and was then the largest building in the city to be built of quarried granite. Standing on the south side of on the site of Provost Thomas Menzies' "stane hoose"—it is now the head office of the Bank of Scotland (see Chapter 15).

With the prospect of expansion, the magistrates of Aberdeen thought it expedient to make a new appointment— Superintendent of the Town's Works, later to be styled City Architect. Their foresight in selecting John Smith (1781-

1852) for the post is one of the most fortunate steps ever taken in the city's history. John Smith was the son of William (''Sink'em'') Smith, a highly skilled builder, with whom he served his apprenticeship. Later, John went to London where he studied under several of the leading architects of the day. While resident in England, he developed a strong attachment to the Tudor style of architecture—hence his byname ''Tudor Johnny''. John Smith was an exceptionally talented man and thoroughly practical. He had a fine sense of design and planning and was possessed of a very wide vision. The list of buildings to his credit in Aberdeen and in the north-east is indeed an impressive one and it is to be regretted that, within recent years, so many of them have been demolished—notably Sir Alexander Bannerman's house (1810), later the Royal Northern Club in Union Street, the first building to be erected west of Union Bridge (1805) and Smith's first work in the city.

In some measure, John Smith has been eclipsed by his younger professional rival Archibald Simpson (1790-1847) who has enjoyed a far wider publicity. Both men were fine architects but John Smith had a more balanced viewpoint and on several occasions was the restraining influence when Simpson's unreasonable dislike of everything from the past demanded wholesale demolition—the historic Bridge of Dee being a notable example. That Simpson had little time for any of his predecessors' work is obvious from records of his day.

Archibald Simpson was the son of William Simpson, a well-to-do tailor and outfitter in the Broadgate—the firm eventually became Simpson & Whyte. His mother was Barbara Dauney, from whose family he inherited his art and love of music. She was the sister of William Dauney, architect, the man responsible for guiding his nephew's early steps in the profession. Dauney was a man of refined tastes, as the house he designed for the Simpson family in the Guestrow showed. Unfortunately, this delightful dwelling was demolished in the clearance following the First World War.

In 1804, Simpson was apprenticed to James Massie, architect and builder. Five years later, he went to London and entered the office of Robert Lugar, then enjoying a run of popularity as a country gentleman's architect. Lugar was the author of four books on domestic architecture and it is clear that these monographs made a deep impression on young Simpson for most of his domestic work in the city and surrounding district may be traced to Lugar's publications. Before returning to Aberdeen in 1814, Simpson visited Florence and Rome.

The architectural trend at this time was the adaption of Classic forms to modern uses, the Grecian style being then in vogue. The hard, crystalline granite was ideal for this style of building—as both Smith and Simpson found. John Smith's Town's Schools (1841) in Little Belmont Street, now part of Aberdeen Academy, and Archibald Simpson's front to the Music Hall (1820), are excellent examples of the period. Neither Smith nor Simpson excelled when they worked in the Gothic style.

One of the most fascinating streets of this period is Adelphi Court, laid out in 1815 on the levelled summit of St. Catherine's Hill. Several of the original houses still stand, their wide and dignified entrance doorways with their elaborate fanlights recalling those tranquil days of the sedan chair when a ''fare'' was ''collected'' or ''set down'' within the entrance vestibule of the house.

Among the most impressive buildings erected at this time were The Athenaeum (1819) and the North Bank (1839)— now the head office of the Clydesdale Bank Ltd.—both standing in Castle Street and both by Archibald Simpson. John Smith's finely-proportioned screen to St. Nicholas Churchyard in Union Street was built in 1830.

The Disruption in the Church of Scotland in 1843— unfortunate though it was—brought in its wake a building boom in church architecture, but as funds were strictly limited, the architects reverted to less expensive materials and accordingly many of our Disruption churches are of sandstone or even brick. The familiar brick spire of East and Belmont Church—originally shared by three Disruption churches—was built in 1844 by Archibald Simpson. Never an original designer, Simpson took as his model one of the twin spires of the great Gothic church of St. Elizabeth in Marburg, Germany.

James Matthews (1820-1898) was assistant to Archibald Simpson and succeeded to his practice but obviously did not share his former chief's enthusiasm for the Classic styles. In 1853, Balmoral Castle had been built for Queen Victoria by William Smith (1817-1891)—who joined his father "Tudor Johnny" in business—and so Scottish Baronial became the vogue. Accordingly, in 1861, Matthews built the Aberdeen Grammar School and this was followed by the Palace Hotel (now demolished), Rubislaw Terrace, and a number of mansion houses. In 1863—in the same style—William Smith built the Militia Barracks in King Street (now the Corporation's Transport Garages), while two years later the Municipal Buildings were erected by Messrs. Peddie & Kinnear of Edinburgh. In 1893, the Salvation Army Citadel was built by James Soutter, and in 1907 the General Post Office in Crown Street—a truly remarkable achievement.

About this time, the work of a famous London architect —William Butterfield (1814-1900)—was attracting attention and his lavish use of variegated materials in ecclesiastical architecture was shattering the purists. In 1862, this innovation reached Aberdeen when St. Mary's Episcopal Church in Carden Place was built in the Butterfield idiom by Alexander Ellis. It was immediately and aptly styled "The Tartan Kirkie". Ellis's assistant, John Bridgeford Pirie (1852-1892), who shared his former chief's zeal for the unusual, began practice on his own account in 1877. In 1881 he erected Queen's Cross Church, No. 50 Queen's Road—an essay in "bizarre Gothic", and he was architect of part of Hamilton Place.

The close of the 19th century saw the erection of a number of exceptionally fine granite buildings—the Aberdeen

Savings Bank in Union Terrace (1896) and St. Ninian's Church, Mid Stocket Road (1898) both by William Kelly (1861-1944); Beechgrove Church (1896) by George Watt (1864-1931) of Messrs. Brown & Watt; St. Peter's Episcopal Church, Victoria Road, Torry—an unusual building in red granite setts—by Harold Ogil Tarbolton, erected in 1898; St. Margaret's Convent in the Spital (1898) by Sir Ninian Comper, the famous London architect; and Nos. 6-8 Upperkirkgate by Robert Gordon Wilson—an interesting design based on the Scots College in Paris.

The present century opened with a number of interesting buildings in the "Granite City" tradition among them Nos. 261-263 Union Street (1900) by Arthur H. L. Mackinnon; Nos. 24-25 Union Terrace (1902)—the County Offices—by A. G. Sydney Mitchell of London; Marischal College (1903) —a unique example in Perpendicular Gothic—by Alexander Marshall Mackenzie; the Aberdeen Savings Bank in George Street (1905) by William Kelly; the Masonic Temple in Crown Street (1909) by Harbourne Maclennan; the Prudential Assurance Company building in Crown Street (1910) by Paul Waterhouse of London, a President of the Royal Institute of British Architects; and the National Commercial Bank at 78-80 Union Street (1936) by Messrs. Jenkins and Marr— possibly the last of the monumental granite buildings to be erected in the city.

The first of the modern buildings was Telephone House, Bon-Accord Street. Built in 1908 by the well-known London architect Leonard Stokes, it pointed the way towards a modern "Granite City"—but in vain. C. J. Menart's Church of the Sacred Heart, Grampian Road, Torry (1911) also showed a veering from traditional building in Aberdeen, and this was followed by A. B. Gardiner's impressive block of flats in Rosemount.

The final break with the "Granite City" tradition came after the Second World War when concrete—and economy— dictated architectural design and granite declined to the level of an ancillary. Up to the 1930s most architectural firms in the city could claim "descent" from either John Smith or Archibald Simpson, the co-creators of "The Granite City", but twenty years later this potent link in the chain of tradition had been broken.

Today, we have what is called "contemporary architecture". No doubt posterity will find a more appropriate name for it and assess its merit without fear of contradiction. In looking at these structures, the words of Freidrich von Schelling come to mind . . . . "Architecture in general is frozen music". How true! We live in the age of *musique concrete*.

34

THE PECULIAR HAND OF PROVIDENCE

"For all sad words of tongue or pen,
The saddest are these: 'It might have been'."
—John Greenleaf Whittier.

ABOUT twelve miles north-west from Aberdeen and standing within the ancient lordship of the Garioch, is the hamlet of Kinmuck. Although so near the city, Kinmuck is one of the most retired communities in Aberdeenshire and appears to have been so since the dawn of history. Its name is derived from the Gaelic *ceann muc*—"pig's head"—but the significance is obscure.

Kinmuck has a fascinating history. Tradition tells that it was the site of a great struggle between the Scots and the Danes and points to several local names as proof. At all events, the lands of Kinmuck were included in the lordship of the Garioch created by William the Lion (1165-1214) and conferred by him on his younger brother David, Earl of Huntingdon. In the year 1195, Earl David, who took part in the Third Crusade—he was the prototype for Sir Walter Scott's hero in *The Talisman*—made over certain of his Garioch lands to the Abbey of Lindores in Fife and this gift included Kinmuck. The same year, a Bull by Pope Celestine III, confirmed the gift and so, for close upon four centuries, Kinmuck was held by the Church of Rome.

> *Facing.* 1. Quaker Meeting House, Kinmuck.
> 2. Ruined homestead of Achtavan.

1

2

1

2

The Reformation came and by the middle of the 16th century the disintegration of the Lindores property in the Garioch had begun.   In 1596, Kinmuck was purchased by Alexander Irvine of Drum while about the same time William Forbes of Craigievar acquired the neighbouring property of Fintray, part of which lies contiguous to Kinmuck.   Thus these Church lands passed into the hands of two Aberdeenshire lairds.

The story of Kinmuck now moves to Edinburgh where on Tuesday, 8th October, 1657, "His Highness's Council in Scotland" ordered one George Fox to appear before it.   From contemporary records we learn that he "appeared accordingly" when he was ordered to "depart the Nation of Scotland by that day Sevenight".   He declined to do so and records tell that Fox "knowing his Commission to be from God, was carried above the Fear of Man" and the "peculiar hand of Providence was sometimes visible in the manner of his Deliverance".   Thus the tenets of Quakerism were brought to Scotland.

Five years after the incident, an open-air meeting was held on the bleak slopes of Blair Hussey at Kinmuck.   It was a small gathering assembled to hear one of George Fox's followers, Patrick Livingstone of Montrose.   From this humble gathering of Quakers sprang the Kinmuck Meeting which grew to be one of the largest in the country.

The reason for the selection of Kinmuck as a meeting place for the Quakers is not far to seek.   As already mentioned, it was a retired area where meetings could be held without interference.   Several neighbouring lairds were already converts to Quakerism, among them Alexander Jaffray of Ardtannies, Alexander Skene of Newtyle, Alexander Forbes of Aquhorthies and Cairnbrogie, and Alexander Skene of Dyce—all these properties being within a ten-mile radius of Kinmuck.

Facing.   1. Arms of Conn of Auchry.

2. Mary Bannerman's will.

L

Although the Quaker interest in Kinmuck commenced in the year 1662, it was not until 1680 that the Society of Friends finally settled in the area. In that year, a Quaker school-master John Robertson, received a charter from Sir John Forbes of Craigievar and Fintray—the famous "Red Sir John"—conveying to him a piece of land known as "Allan's Croft" lying on the north side of the Fintray—Keith-hall road, while in 1710 he received a second charter—from Alexander Irvine of Drum—of a "yaird and littel toft of land" situated on the south side of the same road opposite "Allan's Croft". Here, the Quakers established themselves and grew in strength until the turn of the 19th century. Thereafter came a gradual decline followed by complete extinction.

Despite the fact that Kinmuck is no longer a Quaker community, there is much to be seen in the hamlet which takes one back to the far-off days when such great figures as Robert Barclay of Ury—"The Apologist", Alexander Jaffray of Kingswells, provost of Aberdeen, and others worshipped at Kinmuck. The Quakers' school and school-house, built in 1681, still stands and of course the Meeting House erected in 1710 to designs by George Wines of Inverurie. Perhaps the most poignant reminder of Quakerism in Kinmuck is the "burial-yaird" at the south-east corner of "Allan's Croft". In the early days of the Society of Friends the erecting of stones was not considered compatible with their beliefs so that the headstones in the "yaird" belong chiefly to the 19th and present centuries. In accordance with Quaker practice, all the headstones—with the exception of one erected without permission—are of uniform pattern for it is held there should be no distinction in death.[15]

But if there is no distinction in their headstones, many of these Quakers have brought distinction and made history. Here, for example, are the headstones of Amos and Anthony Cruickshank—sons of Sarah and John Cruickshank of Balhagardy—who died in 1895 and 1879 respectively. The names of these brothers, the Cruickshanks of Seatiton —now spelt Sittyton—are household words wherever shorthorn cattle breeders foregather. They possessed the largest herd of shorthorn cattle in the world. Then there are the headstones of the Brantinghams—a well-known family of hosiers, and the Wighans—silk manufacturers—some of whom travelled widely in the cause of Quakerism. One of this remarkable family was Amos Wighan, farmer in Kinmuck, who is noted in the Friends' records as being the first Conscientious Objector. In 1803, he received a Charge for the Militia but declining to serve or find a substitute, was promptly fined. The local bailiff came to collect the fine which appears to have been paid in kind for records tell he made off with "two fat bullocks". Another of these Kinmuck headstones bears the name of Peter Brownie who died in 1886. At one stage in his career, Brownie was a notorious resurrectionist who kept medical students well supplied with bodies for dissection, his main source of supply coming from the neighbouring kirk-yards. Despite the strictest surveillance, Peter Brownie was never caught at his nefarious work and eventually repented, becoming a respected member of the Kinmuck Meeting.

In the year 1860, a prophecy was made shortly before her death by Mary Gray, a well-known Kinmuck Quakeress. She foretold the resurgence of the Society of Friends in the district and her prophecy was firmly believed by the surviving Quakers there. It was recalled by her son shortly before his death in 1903. However, the last of the old line of Quakers died at Kinmuck in 1945 and today the "burial-yaird" is the sole possession of the Society of Friends in the area.

> *"Truly the vision tarrieth, but times and*
> *seasons are in the Lord's own keeping."*

35

G L E N   O F   T H E   H I G H   W A T E R

"It's a maxim of a wise man never to return
by the same road he came, providing another's
free to him."

—Sir Walter Scott.

ONE of the most interesting little glens in the Grampians, and certainly one of the most remote, is Glen Fearder. It lies above Balmoral, quite close to the valley of the Dee and almost parallel to it, yet Fearder is entirely cut off from Deeside by the massive bulk of Meal Alvie.

Glen Fearder is a truly mysterious region possessing a strange fascination for those susceptible to atmosphere and it is here, near the head of the glen—"the Glen of the High Water"—that H.M. Queen Elizabeth, The Queen Mother, has a favourite shiel. It is a wild and romantic Highland glen where the Gaelic lingers in its place-names—descriptive names of unusual interest today.

The ancient hill-road running through Glen Fearder is one of the three leading from upper Deeside to Loch Builg, the others being the Bealach Dearg—the Red Pass—from Inver-cauld and the Glen Gairn road—later a military road—from Crathie. The three routes converge at Loch Builg and there-after proceed northwards as a bridle-path to Inchrory and from thence to Tomintoul.

In early records and maps of the district, the Fearder hill-road is frequently referred to as the *Moine an Tighearn* road— "the laird's moss road"—for, at a height of 2,000 feet, it

148

skirts that weirdly desolate stretch of moorland where the lairds of Monaltrie were wont to cast their peats. While the Bealach Dearg and the Glen Gairn road were the most popular routes from Upper Deeside into Banffshire, the Glen Fearder road had its special devotees. These were the wild and lawless caterans, cattle-rievers and illicit whisky-runners, for the secluded nature of the glen rendered it an ideal route for their particular "trades".

At its lower end, Glen Fearder may be approached either from the *Keiloch*—"the narrow field"—or from Inver, originally Inverfearder, but both ways lead to the flat, rather marshy valley of the *Felagie*—"slow burn"—which flows eastwards to meet the Fearder at Ballachlaggan. Almost completely encircled by great pine-covered heights—Craig na Spaine, Meal Alvie, Craig Leek and Meall Gorm, the valley of the *Felagie* is known as Aberarder. It has a fascinating history.

Aberarder was originally possessed by the feudal Earls of Mar who held it direct from the Crown. For several centuries, their tenants and sub-tenants in Aberarder—each of whom held "ane Davoch and two Oxgates" of land—were the Farquharsons of Invercauld and their kinsmen the Shaws of Rothiemurchus. It would seem, however, that in those far off days, life in Aberarder was no sinecure for, besides the Farquharsons and the Shaws, there were no fewer than nineteen "bonnet lairds" residing in the area—all of them living in a state of perpetual warfare with one another, or with some common enemy. At long length, the exasperated Farquharsons, as Mar's chief tenants, decided to take decisive action. They invited the nineteen "bonnet-lairds" to meet them in the "gryt barn at Abirardir" where the Farquharsons summarily "justiced" eighteen of them by hanging them from the roof-tree. The nineteenth "bonnet-laird" escaped but a document of the time states briefly that he gave no further trouble. After the Jacobite Rising of 1715, when the Mar Estates were forfeited, Aberarder was acquired in 1731 by the Farquharsons of Invercauld who still own the property.

Less than a century ago, Aberarder was a flourishing community—today it is almost completely depopulated. The people have gone from the land but evidence of their existence is everywhere to be seen—ruined farms, crofts, huts and sheilings, enclosed fields and signs of cultivation at a much higher level than practised today. A few of the original holdings remain such as Balmore—tenanted by the Shaws of Rothiemurchus as far back as the 16th century. It was from this remarkable family that a number of noted men derived —Sir John Macdonald, Prime Minister of Canada, Dr. Andrew Robertson of Indego, Queen Victoria's Commissioner at Balmoral, and of course the celebrated John Brown, Queen Victoria's personal highland attendant.

Above Balmore, the Glen Fearder hill-road crosses the swift-flowing Fearder Burn and proceeds up the left bank of that stream. It passes through delightful birch woods—the haunt of black-cock and pheasant—and rises steeply as it skirts the western shoulder of Creag Bheag. Here, on a knoll high above the Fearder, stands the ruined holding of Ratlich —obviously a place of some distinction in its day. It too was tenanted by the Shaws of Rothiemurchus.

A short distance above Ratlich, the Fearder alters the direction of its course and is here joined by the *Allt Cul—* "burn of the corner". About a mile above this point, the headwaters of the Fearder are reached—the *Allt Guish*, the "burn of the fire" and the *Allt Chlie*—the "left-hand burn". The confluence of these two streams was originally known as *Auchnagymlinn*, a name now obsolete and its meaning obscure.

The last habitation in Glen Fearder is Auchtavan, mentioned in early charters as "Achdavend, a pendicle of Balmor". Now quite remote, Auchtavan was for centuries tenanted by the Rothiemurchus Shaws whose rental was paid in kind as the name of the holding implies. Auchtavan is derived from the Gaelic meaning "the field of the two kids". Thus, in accordance with feudal custom, the rental paid to the laird for tenancy of Auchtavan was two young goats.

Well-sheltered from the cold north winds by Creag Bhalg, Auchtavan is fully 1,500 feet above sea level. It commands an extensive and fantastically beautiful panorama to the south —to Lochnagar and the other high-tops—and is possibly the grandest view on Deeside, especially in winter or in early spring. It is clear that Auchtavan was a holding of some extent as indicated by the ruinous ''laigh-biggins'' many of which contain unique constructional features seldom seen today.

The Glen Fearder hill-road by-passes Auchtavan and after crossing the already-mentioned *Moine an Tighearn*—''laird's moss''—descends into the valley of the Gairn where it joins the bridle-path to Inchrory and Tomintoul at lonely Loch Builg.

36

ABERDEENSHIRE CARDINAL

"One here will constant be,
come wind, come weather."

—John Bunyan.

IN the Aberdeenshire parish of Monquhitter, about five-and-a-half miles east-north-east from the township of Turriff, lies the farm of Castle of Auchry—so named on account of there having stood on, or near, the site of the farm buildings, an ancient stronghold. The lands of Auchry—originally called Fintry—formed part of the extensive territories owned by the powerful family of Hay, Earls of Erroll and hereditary High Constables of Scotland.

Sometime in the 15th century—and probably during the lifetime of William Hay, 3rd Earl of Erroll—there settled on the lands of Auchry, a younger son of Donald, 2nd Lord of the Isles, chief of the clan Macdonald, and his wife Mary Leslie, daughter of Sir Andrew Leslie. This son was William who assumed the surname Conn—from the legendary founder of his clan "Conn of the Battles"—and was the first Conn of Auchry. William's settlement at Auchry was under the aegis of the Hays and is said to have been largely due to his exceptional abilities as a master-mason.

By the year 1552, the Conns had established themselves in Monquhitter and had erected at Auchry for their own occupation, a modest stronghold—"Red Castle", so called, no doubt from the colour of the sandstone used in its building. In addition to this, the Conns of Auchry are credited

152

with the building of the neighbouring castles of Gight (*circa* 1550), Delgaty (1570), and Towie-Barclay (1593). It is possible they also built Craig Castle (*circa* 1560) in the parish of Auchindoir.

However, skilled as they were, it is not as castle-builders that the Conns of Auchry are known in history, but as champions of the ancient Faith, notably George who rose to be a figure of international fame.

George Conn was a son of Patrick Conn, 4th of Auchry, by his wife Margaret Cheyne, daughter of Thomas Cheyne of Esslemont in Aberdeenshire. He was born at Auchry in 1598 and when about fifteen years of age was sent to the Roman Catholic College at Douai in France. From Douai he went to Rome and from there to the University of Bologna where he completed his education. It was during his sojourn at Bologna that Conn reached the turning point in his astonishing career.

George Conn, quite apart from his learning and undoubted ability, appears to have possessed great personal charm for, throughout his life, he had the happy knack of making friends and of making them quickly. Thus, while a student at Bologna, he attracted the attention of the powerful Duke of Mirandola who invited him to become tutor to his sons, an appointment which terminated in the summer of 1623 when Conn became attached to the household of Cardinal Monalto. Conn's unusual qualities were soon recognised by the Cardinal who on his death some six months later, left a considerable legacy to the young Scot. The following year—in 1624—George Conn published his first book *Vita Mariae Stuartae*. This work on Scotland's tragic queen was re-published in Wurzburg a year later.

We next hear of him as secretary to Cardinal Barberini when he accompanied the latter on his missions to France and Spain as Papal Nuncio. Barberini was a nephew of the Pope—Urban XIII—and it is therefore not surprising to find Conn appointed domestic prelate to the Pope, created Canon of St. Lorenzo's Church at Damaso in Rome and enriched with other benefices. Conn, or Coneas, as he is generally called, was now rising to fame and power.

It was not, however, until 1636 that the name of George Conn was heard in this country. For some time, the appointment of a new Papal Nuncio to Protestant Britain had been under consideration. The post, hitherto held by Panzani, was no sinecure and it was essential that the right man be selected. This man was George Conn who landed at Rye in February, 1636.

He was an immediate success with Charles I (1625-1649) and with his consort Henrietta Maria (1609-1669), younger daughter of Henry IV of France, by his second wife Marie de Medici. He was also extremely popular at Court—for again his great personal charm won him friends—and what was more important to the Vatican—converts in high places. His most valuable convert was the Lady Newport, for this great lady's conversion raised a storm of protest led by Archbishop Laud who demanded that King Charles should enforce Protestant law. But the king thought otherwise and Conn continued as the Vatican's popular Nuncio until 1639 when his health gave way and he received permission to return to Italy. George Conn clearly foresaw the coming "Troubles" but left the country before the storm broke and it was his successor Rossetti who had to face the problems which ended so tragically for both king and country.

Conn set out for Rome a very sick man but died on the way in 1640 having reached the city of Genoa. His mission to Britain had been conspicuously successful and Pope Urban VIII designated him Cardinal. However, Conn died before receiving his Cardinal's hat and was buried in the Church of St. Lorenzo in Damaso, Rome, where a memorial was erected to him by his patron Cardinal Barberini.

The Conns of Auchry, on account of their adherence to their Faith, suffered very considerably at the time of the Reformation and during the "Troubles". In 1690 George Conn's father, Patrick Conn, 4th of Auchry, was living in Paris in much reduced circumstances. Eventually, the Conns removed to Spain where their descendants are said to still reside. In the Registers of the various continental Roman Catholic Colleges, the names of several of the Conn family appear, among them Father Alexander Conn of Auchry who became Superior of the Scottish Mission.

The old "Red Castle" of Auchry gradually disintegrated and today only a few fragments survive to remind us of the Conn's sojourn in these parts. Built into the farm buildings at Castle of Auchry, they consist of part of an altar recess, elaborately carved, and bearing the initials "I. H. S." (*Jesus Hominum Salvator*), and the family's armorial bearings—the arms of Patrick Conn, 4th of Auchry, impaled with those of his wife Margaret Cheyne of Esslemont, *viz.*: "A fess engrailed between two crescents in chief, and a buckle in base (for Conn); and, 1st and 4th, three cross crosslets fitchée (for Cheyne), 2nd and 3rd, three edock leaves slipped (for Marischal); supporters, two "cons" (squirrels), with the motto *Constant and Kynd.*

37

THE ELUSIVE COFFIN

"Care to our coffin adds a nail, no doubt,
And ev'ry grin, so merry, draws one out."
—Peter Pindar.

HOW the fantastic rumour regarding the final resting place of Mary Bannerman, a lady of quality who died in Aberdeen early in the 18th century originated, has never been explained.

Mary Bannerman was the eldest daughter of Alexander Bannerman of Elsick in Kincardineshire, and his wife Marion Hamilton of East Binning. Mary, who had three sisters and four brothers, married George Leslie, 4th of Findrassie in Morayshire, and it was after her husband's death in 1692 that she came to live permanently in Aberdeen—in a "back-tenement" of the Guestrow, then the fashionable quarter of the burgh.

Usually referred to as "Lady Findrassie", Mary Bannerman eventually became a Quaker. At what point in her life she joined the Society of Friends is uncertain but it would appear to have been shortly after her husband's death although many of her life-long friends and neighbours such as the Barclays of Ury, near Stonehaven, and the Burnetts of Muchalls were prominently associated with the Society. Her near neighbour in the Guestrow, George Forbes of Brux on Donside, was also a leading Quaker and of course the Friends' Meeting House then stood in the Guestrow—in Quakers' Court, north of, and adjacent to Provost Skene's House.

In the year 1704, Mary Bannerman "knowing that Death is most certain to all and the tyme of it uncertain" made her will which was witnessed by five well-known Quakers including Andrew Jaffray of Kingswells and George Forbes of Brux. It was at this juncture that the rumour appears to have started for in her Will, Mary Bannerman left her house—the "back-tenement" in the Guestrow—to the Society of Friends, rumour maintaining she willed her house on condition that the Quakers "kept her embalmed body on the premises". This fantastic rumour, once circulated, persisted down the years and two centuries later was the means of causing considerable embarrassment.

In her will, Mary Bannerman expresses quite clearly her wishes regarding the disposal of her body which renders the rumour all the more baffling. She specifies "plain Grave-cloaths without any maner of vain superflous attire" and requests "a plaine Coffine without any mulloring, carving or collowring, and that no mortcloath of any collour be put thereupon". She then directs "it be carried to the Friends' burial place in the Gallowgate at Aberdeine if I dye there or near it and that ther be no mowrning habites nor crapes used by any of my Relations".

However, despite these precise instructions, the burial records of the Gallowgate graveyard make no mention of Mary Bannerman having been interred there, nor does her name appear in any of the other Quaker burial-ground records. Could it be that this fanned the flame of rumour?

At all events, Mary Bannerman's Will makes interesting reading especially in regard to her effects in "the hous in the Ghostraw of Aberdein". These include what is called "ane complete bedding—ane feather bedd, one bolster, two pillows, two pairs of plaides and ane faike (small cover), ane pair of sheets and ane covering with hangings about the bedd and ane chamber pot". Most of the articles specified, Mary Bannerman gave to her friends but she directs that the "eight wandscott chairs in the hall" be delivered to her brother-in-law whom she styles "Fyndrassie".

But what of the rumour regarding Mary Bannerman's burial? For two centuries it lingered on but with the demolition of the Guestrow in the 1920s it was revived and gained currency. A perfervid historian made diligent search for the elusive coffin containing the mummified remains of "Lady Findrassie". Success crowned his efforts and he located the stone coffin built into the wall of her former home.

In due course, Quakers residing in Aberdeen were notified that Mary Bannerman's coffin was to be lifted and that her mortal remains could then be taken to some suitable place of interment. Consequently, on a chill November morning, a number of Quakers foregathered among the ruins of Mary Bannerman's house in the Guestrow to receive her remains. The coffin was lifted carefully and lowered to the ground. They looked in—then at each other—and finally at the historian. It was empty. The awful silence was broken by the mason in charge of operations, a practical man of forthright speech, who forcibly exploded the Mary Bannerman rumour for all time—"Yon's nae a coffin, it's a soo's troch!"

38

SPARK OF GENIUS

"Art is a jealous mistress."
—Emerson.

ABERDEEN has produced relatively few artists and fewer great sculptors. This is perhaps surprising when one recalls the remarkable stone-carvings executed here during the 16th and 17th centuries and the subsequent rise and development of the granite industry. However, the few sculptors cradled in the city have certainly left their mark and achieved distinction far beyond the "twal' mile roon".

One of these Aberdeen sculptors was Alexander Brodie who, over a century ago—in the summer of 1864—began work on a commission which was to carry him to the forefront of his profession, a full-length figure of Queen Victoria portraying Her Majesty as "Queen of Scots". It was the opportunity of a life-time and Brodie made the most of it.

Alexander Brodie belonged to a family having its origins in Banff where, for several generations, they had been engaged in fishing. His father, John Brodie (1787-1865), was no exception while his mother Mary Walker (1786-1846) also came of fishing stock. John and Mary Brodie were married about the year 1814 and while living in Banff had a family of two sons and a daughter—William, John and Christina. On the death of the latter, the Brodies moved from Banff to Aberdeen. This was in 1821 when they made their home in Aberdeen's fishing quarter—at No. 6 Garvock Wynd, Fittie. Here, their third son was born in 1829—Alexander Brodie, the future sculptor.

William, the eldest of the Brodie brothers also became a sculptor—and a famous one—while John followed the family tradition and went to sea. Nothing is known of his career beyond the fact that he was drowned off Quebec in 1846.

Early in life, William Brodie learned that while dexterity in art had its place, it was more important to know "the right people". Consequently, he moved to Edinburgh where he executed literally hundreds of busts of the prominent people of the day and, as one would expect, was elected to full membership of the Royal Scottish Academy. He never returned to Aberdeen and died in Edinburgh in 1881. Although William Brodie was much less talented than his younger brother Alexander, he reaped all the monetary and academic rewards of his profession.

There is little doubt that Alexander Brodie was, in his early years, influenced by his elder brother, but their careers had nothing in common for, while William "lived it up" in Edinburgh "society", Alexander worked doggedly away in his own home town with little or no encouragement to prosecute his art. After attending school, Alexander Brodie became apprenticed to a brass-finisher and it was at this stage of his career that the public-spirited Sheriff Watson took an interest in young Alexander's future—as indeed he had done in the case of the elder brother William. Through the Sheriff's influence and financial assistance, Alexander was enabled to study sculpture in Edinburgh and in England but in 1851 he returned to Aberdeen. Here, in a studio in Justice Street, Alexander Brodie set up as a sculptor.

At the outset of his career he had to be content with small commissions and the first of these was a memorial tablet to the Rev. Robert Forbes of Woodside—a chaste example of Brodie's skill. This was followed by similar commissions which kept the young sculptor in funds. Alexander worked chiefly in marble but the rigours of the north-east's climate

Facing. 1. Priest Gordon, Nelson Street.

2. Cast iron "pig" at Gairlochy burial ground.

1

2

1

2

have taken their toll and in consequence several of his most charming works in the city's older churchyards are badly weathered. The simple obelisk he designed to the memory of his parents stands over their grave in the burial-ground of East St. Clement's Church—Fittie Kirk, which the Brodies attended.

In the year 1860 came Alexander's first big opportunity to show his genius. He was commissioned to execute a full-length figure of a popular Aberdeen clergyman, the much-loved Priest Gordon. This fine figure, carried out in granite, may be seen at St. Peter's Roman Catholic School in Nelson Street—it long adorned the old school in Constitution Street —and greatly enhanced the sculptor's reputation.

Brodie was now making his way and the Priest Gordon commission was followed by another—a figure of the Duke of Gordon for the Square at Huntly. Thus, in the summer of 1864, Alexander Brodie, whose talents had attracted the notice of Prince Albert, was commissioned by the City of Aberdeen to execute a full-length figure in Sicilian marble of Queen Victoria as the "Queen of Scots" to stand at the important corner of Union Street and St. Nicholas Street. The figure was beautifully designed and exquisitely cut but the material did not stand up to the Aberdeen climate and in 1888, the figure was removed to the Town House vestibule where it stands today in the staircase well, its great beauty of line completely unseen on account of its appalling position. A substitute figure in bronze by C. B. Birch—now at Queen's Cross—was placed at the corner of St. Nicholas Street.

Unhappily, the Queen Victoria commission was Alexander Brodie's last great work for, overburdened by commissions, his mind became deranged and on 29th May, 1867, he attempted to take his own life. Alexander Brodie died the following day and was laid to rest with his parents in Fittie Kirk-yard.

Facing.   1. Stone font from Forvie Kirk.
        2. *Titian's first essay in colour*, Aberdeen Art Gallery.

161

39

SASUNNACH CRIME

"His skirts be verie shorte,
with pleates set thick about."
—Derrick.

DURING the past hundred years, many important books have been written on Highland dress. This has resulted in the accumulation of a very considerable amount of valuable information relative to the subject; has focussed attention on it and added glamour to what was originally a very simple and strictly utilitarian garment.

Most books on Highland dress make some passing reference to a certain Thomas Rawlinson, a remote almost legendary figure in 18th century Scotland, who with the passing years, tends to become more and more obscure. He is still an enigma in the Highlands and even today there are Scotsmen who would prefer not to mention his name. In their eyes, Rawlinson committed an unpardonable ''crime''—and he was a *Sasunnach*.

From the evidence, it is quite certain that Thomas Rawlinson did not commit his ''crime'' with malice aforethought— his was a sudden inspiration, an emergency measure, which proved successful and snowballed as does many another innovation. Curiously enough, although historians have been aware of Rawlinson's ''crime'', surprisingly little has been written about the ''criminal'' whose brief sojourn in the Highlands gained for him a unique place in Scottish annals.

162

The story begins eleven years after the Jacobite Rising of 1715. The Highlands of Scotland were then under military control and certain regions, hitherto looked upon as hostile, were now beginning to be regarded as comparatively safe. One of these areas was the Great Glen where General George Wade was carrying out his vast programme of road building. This combination of circumstances—military protection and improved access—offered unusual prospects for development and so, for the first time in history, the Highlands of Scotland were being opened up to commercial enterprise.

In the centre of the Great Glen, and branching from it to the north-west, is wild and beautiful Glen Garry. From an early date, Glen Garry had been owned by the Macdonells, descendants of Archibald, second son of John, 7th Lord of the Isles. The Macdonells had their home at Invergarry Castle, a picturesque, fortified tower-house, crowning the rugged *Creag-an-fitheach* — "Rock-of-the-raven" — on the north-western shores of Loch Oich.

During the Jacobite Rising of 1715, the Macdonells of Glen Garry supported the Stuarts as a result of which, Alistair the 11th chief, was outlawed and heavily fined while his stronghold—Invergarry Castle—was burned by Government troops. The Rising had greatly impoverished the Macdonells so that their only remaining asset was the well-wooded stretch of country from which they derived their title. Prospects for the future seemed grim indeed. However, John Macdonell, then living in Inverness in straitened circumstances, had an unexpected stroke of good fortune—an offer which he was quick to accept, despite its source—from England.

The scene now moves south to another mountainous region of great beauty fully three hundred miles distant from Glen Garry—to the English Lake District. One of the oldest families in Westmoreland are the Rawlinsons, the "sons of Rolland". The first of the family to be mentioned in history are two doughty warrior brothers, Walter and Henry Rawlinson, who distinguished themselves at Agincourt in 1415 and became gentlemen of coat armour. From the elder brother, Walter, derived Thomas Rawlinson, father of Alexander, one of the princely Abbots of Furness. Now, the Abbot's cousin and heiress was Margaret Rawson of York, wife of William Sandys of Furness Fells. Thus, on the dissolution of the monastries in England, part of the assets of Furness Abbey—three important bloomsmithies—passed to William Sandys and his neighbour John Sawrey whose widow subsequently married John Rawlinson of Greenhead. It was through this marriage that the Rawlinsons eventually acquired Graythwaite Hall, which became the principal seat of the family, and from Sawrey's interest in Furness Abbey bloomsmithies originated the Rawlinsons' association with the iron industry of Furness.

Thomas, the first Rawlinson of Graythwaite and Rusland, was born in 1574. He married Bridget Sawrey by whom he had a family of three, the elder son William succeeding to Graythwaite and Rusland. In the military tradition of his family, William Rawlinson raised a regiment of Furness Volunteers and as its captain, fought at Marston Moor and Ribble Bridge. William married his kinswoman, Elizabeth Sawrey, by whom he had a large family. His eldest son was born in 1627 and would have succeeded to the family estate but for the fact that he became a Quaker. On account of his adherence to the new faith, Thomas was disowned by his father. He later became a close friend of George Fox, Margaret and Henry Fell, James Nayler and other prominent Quakers, sharing in all their trials and privations. In 1663, Thomas Rawlinson married Dorothy Hutton of Rampside, by whom he had a family of ten. The most noted of this Quaker family was Lydia, who in 1706 married Bryan Lancaster of Kendal. Lydia was the first of the Rawlinsons to visit Scotland and doubtless influenced her nephew, Thomas Rawlinson, in his Highland venture.

Thomas Rawlinson was the eldest son of William—the brother of Lydia—and his wife Margaret Goulding of Chippenham. He was born at Graythwaite Hall in the year 1689. Brought up in a strict Quaker atmosphere, Thomas, at the age of ten and through the will of his great-uncle John Rawlinson, barrister-at-law, succeeded to the Whittington Hall estate, the succession being conditional on his conforming to the Church of England. Thomas conformed, and accordingly became a man of considerable means. In 1718, he married Elizabeth Darrand of Lutterworth, by whom he had an only child Judith. Although without any practical knowledge, Thomas, like so many of the Rawlinson family, was greatly interested in the iron industry and its development. He was a man of unusual vision and energy and, of course, possessed of the means whereby he could find outlet for his abilities. Thus, in 1726, Thomas Rawlinson launched a project for the smelting of iron, not, as one might expect, in the Furness district so long associated with the iron industry —but in the remote Highlands of Scotland. Consequently, in March, 1727, Thomas Rawlinson of Whittington Hall entered into an agreement with John Macdonell, 12th chief of Glen Garry, its purpose being the "Trade and Business of Pigg and other Iron".

The selection of Glen Garry as the locus for Rawlinson's iron smelting foundry was, of course, due to the unusual wealth of timber in the locality as stated in the agreement "All and every Woods standing, growing and lying in and upon the Lands of Glen Garry". To these woods, Rawlinson was guaranteed "peaceful ingress and egress"—a pious hope had he known it—for a period of thirty-one years.

Alas, due to circumstances beyond Rawlinson's control ranging from high freightage and poor quality ore to rapine and murder, the Glen Garry enterprise was a dismal failure. It lasted only seven years. Thomas Rawlinson's difficulties were insuperable, while his ingenuous Quaker character was no match for the wily Macdonells with their inborn duplicity. Actually, had the Highlanders possessed the intelligence to see it, they never had it so good, for, under Rawlinson's guidance, they were provided with steady employment, had good wages, new houses, ample food and drink and many perquisites hitherto unheard of in the Highlands.

Rawlinson was an excellent employer and quite two centuries ahead of his time. His Glen Garry Foundry was organised on a community basis and the improved way of life he introduced was such that, when Rawlinson eventually withdrew to England, nearly two hundred years were to elapse before the standard he set returned to the Highlands.

Although the Highlands of Scotland were nominally under military protection, Thomas Rawlinson's life was frequently threatened as were the lives of several of his English workmen. For example, as part of Rawlinson's agreement with Macdonell, the former undertook to repair Invergarry Castle for his occupation during the run of his lease. However, the idea of a *Sasunnach* living in their chief's stronghold aroused Macdonell's followers to a frenzy and they attempted to murder the unsuspecting Rawlinson—and this while accepting his hospitality.

Despite his Quaker parentage and upbringing, Thomas Rawlinson appears to have been a throwback to his military ancestors for, while living in Glen Garry, his closest friends were drawn from the military personnel at the neighbouring barracks. Among these were General George Wade and Captain Edward Burt, and in Rawlinson's account book are items indicating that he kept open house to the soldiery at Invergarry Castle—"Drinks to Captain Goad's crew"; "Two bottles of *Aqua Vitae* to the Black Watch"; "Treat to Officers at Fort William on King George's birthday"; etc., etc. Rawlinson's gifts were often quite lavish—"A King's Hunting Saddle to Captain Campbell"; "A horse to Glengarry" (Macdonell); "Silver decanters to Lady Glen Garry to strengthen the Company's interest in the Highlands"; and a far-sighted gift "Tip to Sergeant-Major—to prevent workmen enlisting". It was, in a measure, due to Thomas Rawlinson's close associations with the military in the Great Glen that his "crime" was committed.

The first mention of Thomas Rawlinson's "crime" was given in a letter dated 1768. It was written by one, Evan Baillie of Aberriachan. a son of Alexander Baillie of Dochfour, Inverness-shire. The accuracy of Evan Baillie's letter has frequently been challenged, but as Baillie received a very strict legal training in Edinburgh and was subsequently in legal practice in Inverness, one may assume he was a man of integrity. In the letter, Baillie avers he knew Thomas Rawlinson about the year 1728. This statement has been questioned, but Rawlinson himself supplies the proof of the acquaintanceship through his *Accounts for the Year 1729*—legal fees paid by him to Evan Baillie, Clerk of the Peace at Inverness, in connection with the murder of one of Rawlinson's workmen. Baillie describes Rawlinson as a ''man of genius and quick parts'' and asserts ''he became very fond of the Highland dress and wore it in the neatest form''. Proof of this was not forthcoming until nearly a century later.

In 1729, Highland dress consisted of the belted-plaid—*breacan an fheilidh*—a single garment, gathered in and belted at the waist, and covering the upper and lower parts of the body. Composed of a single piece of cloth, twelve ells in length, it was the Highlanders' only garment. Now, Thomas Rawlinson employed many Highlanders in his Glen Garry Foundry, and although he found their dress highly decorative and ideal for the outdoor life they led, it was extremely awkward and much too warm for work in a foundry. To suggest that the Highlanders should discard the belted-plaids during working hours would leave them naked, while the suggestion that they wear trousers—the hated *Sasunnach* costume—would cause trouble on a big scale. Thomas Rawlinson certainly had a problem.

One particularly stormy night, a detachment of soldiers from Fort William sought shelter at Thomas Rawlinson's hospitable fireside at Invergarry Castle. In the party was Private Parkinson, a regimental tailor, who, fresh from England, was fascinated by everything he saw around him, especially the Highland dress. However, while he was discussing the decorative qualities of Highland dress with Rawlinson, a Highlander joined the company. Wet to the skin, he removed his belted-plaid in order to dry it at the fire. Only then did Parkinson realise that it was a single garment.

Rawlinson then explained his problem to the regimental tailor. Would it be possible to make the belted-plaid into two garments, a lower garment pleated as before, but attached to a belt, and an upper garment for use as a cloak or blanket? Parkinson took Rawlinson's measurements, secured a length of tartan—*breacan*, set to work and so the first little-kilt—*feile-beag*—came into being. This was Thomas Rawlinson's terrible "crime"—he had dared to tamper with the ancient dress of the Highlands and he, a *Sasunnach*, had dared to wear it—as Evan Baillie recorded "in the neatest form".

The story of Rawlinson's "crime" was endorsed by Colonel Sir John Sinclair of the Highland Fencibles. This was in 1796, but fifty years were to pass before the full details of the "crime" were made public in *Costumes of the Clans* published in 1845 by the remarkable brothers John Sobieski Stuart and Charles Edward Stuart. The story of the "crime" was first given to the brothers by the Macdonell family with whom they frequently stayed and it was subsequently confirmed by men then living in Glen Garry.

However, Thomas Rawlinson's "crime" proved a most popular one. Macdonell of Glen Garry himself had a little-kilt made for his own use, while Rawlinson ordered a batch for his Highland workmen. These proved an unqualified success and finally the *feile-beag* became the official dress of the Highland Regiments.

By the year 1735, Thomas Rawlinson saw that the end of the Glen Garry Foundry was not far off and the following year he returned to England a very disillusioned man. His project had proved a dismal failure and he had lost over £7,000, a considerable sum at that date. Rawlinson's story is one of heroic endeavour against overwhelming odds. Doubtless, the privations and disappointments he suffered in the Highlands took their toll, for he died in 1737, the year following his return from Glen Garry.

Today, of course, the belted-plaid is a matter of history, while Rawlinson is all but forgotten. Yet his "crime"—the kilt as we know it—becomes increasingly popular with the passing years.

40

BURIED BARONY

"If evyr maydenis malysone
Dyd licht upon drye lande,
Lat nocht bee fund in Furvye's glebys
Bot thystl, bente and sande."

—The curse of Forvie.

THE ancient province of Buchan in Aberdeenshire lies to the north of the River Ythan. It is a comparatively flat, maritime region with few outstanding physical features, yet possessing a certain peculiar charm. The district is largely devoted to farming and fishing.

One of the most remarkable coastal sections of Buchan is Forvie—immediately north of Newburgh—a strangely desolate stretch of sand 1,700 acres in extent where, with varying winds, its contours are constantly changing.

Although Forvie possesses numerous prehistoric remains of unusual interest, its chief claim to attention rests on the fact that below the surface of its drifting sands, there lies a forgotten barony and its village, obliterated four-and-a-half centuries ago in a devastating sand storm. Originally, the barony of Forvie was a parish in its own right but in the 16th century—subsequent to the storm—it was merged with the adjacent parish of Slains. The rent roll of the vanished parish was preserved at Slains Castle until 1830. At all events, in local records of 1654, Forvie is succinctly dismissed as "now overblown".

Many fascinating legends relative to the sand storm which obliterated both barony and village have survived. The first of these would seem to have been that circulated just over a century and a half after the catastrophe, the author of the "account" being one "Maister Masson". In the year 1570, Masson published *The Acts of the Church* wherein he tells that "the folks of Forvie suffered this heavy judgement because they were Papists and grossly ignorant"—he was obviously a keen supporter of the Reformed Church of Scotland. Printed in London in black-letter, "Maister Masson's" publication is now extremely rare—almost as rare as are the facts regarding the calamitous event.

The boundaries of the former barony of Forvie have been variously given but only its eastern and southern marches—the North Sea and the River Ythan—can now be confirmed with certainty. The village stood on both banks of the tiny stream where it enters the North Sea at Rockend, just south of Forvie Ness. Of course, it is no longer possible to determine the extent of the village but from the many bent-covered mounds of sand indicative of former habitations, it would appear to have been a fair-sized one. On the left bank of the stream on an elevated site measuring approximately forty feet long by twenty feet in width, stand the fragmentary remains of Forvie kirk. The kirk was built of stone—at this writing part of the north gable-wall is visible—and it would seem to have been a structure of some architectural distinction. Towards the end of last century, a small, octagonal-shaped font in granite was unearthed from the site and removed to the manse of Slains for preservation. From the burial ground surrounding the ruined church, quantities of human bones have been brought to the surface by continued burrowing of rabbits.

Forvie kirk was founded in the 7th century by St. Adamnan, 9th Abbot of Iona. He is best remembered in Aberdeenshire for his associations with *Brecbannoch* of Monymusk—the beautiful casket made specially to contain a relic of the great St. Columba, now preserved in the National Museum of Antiquities, Edinburgh. Eventually, Forvie kirk passed to the Abbey of Arbroath and following upon the

Reformation, was in 1574 gifted by King James VI (1567-1625) to King's College, Old Aberdeen. In 1766, the patronage of the united churches of Forvie and Slains was sold by the College to James, Lord Boyd, 15th Earl of Erroll, and 19th High Constable of Scotland.

The barony of Forvie formed part of the extensive lands of Slains which were granted by the Crown to Sir Gilbert Hay, 1st High Constable of Scotland, for his services to the country. The identity of the laird of Forvie at the time of the great storm is obscure, but he certainly held the barony from William Hay, 4th High Constable—a nephew of King Robert II (1371-1406)—who died at Forvie in the year 1437. In 1368, Sir Thomas Hay, the 3rd High Constable, had made an agreement with Sir William Fenton of that ilk, by which he granted him certain lands in Slains, but in 1392, Robert III (1390-1406) declined to ratify this and all other grants made by Sir Thomas. It is possible, therefore, that the Fentons were holding Forvie when the catastrophe occurred, but here tradition takes over from recorded history.

The story goes that when the laird of Forvie died—about the year 1391—his three daughters, his co-heiresses, were dispossessed of their Forvie heritage. Accordingly, these "maydenis malysone" were driven from their home and taking ship from Scotland eventually reached France. Once safe "upon drye lande", the unhappy girls—individually and collectively—called down the direst curses on the barony of Forvie as indicated in the "fret" heading this chapter—and they had not long to wait for their revenge.

The great sand storm with its resultant obliteration of the barony and village of Forvie has been variously dated. However, there seems a strong possibility that the calamitous event took place on 18th August, 1413, a day of fantastic climatic phenomena recorded in many parts of the world. For example, on the same day, two widely separated volcanoes erupted simultaneously—Hecla in Iceland and Vesuvius in Italy—while gales of unprecedented fury swept many countries.

In Aberdeen, it is recorded that a great wind from the south-east which lasted many days, blew vast quantities of sand from the mouth of the River Dee north-westwards towards the estuary of the River Don—which then entered the North Sea opposite the Broad Hill—thus completely blocking its opening to the sea. A series of lochs were formed on the Links—the Canny-Sweet-Pots—which remained for many years until the slow-moving river eventually made a new course for itself due east from the Brig o' Balgownie. A somewhat similar tale comes from the parish of Crimond between Peterhead and Fraserburgh. Caught in the gale off Rattray Head, a cargo vessel immediately sought refuge in the small port of Rattray, only to find itself when the storm abated, completely landlocked, a great barrier of sand having blown across the entrance to the port thus forming an extensive sheet of water—the present Loch of Strathbeg. The Cotehill and Sand Lochs at Forvie, each over 15 acres in extent, were formed at the same time.

From the south-east, the unrelenting gale blew over the low-lying barony of Forvie driving before it dense clouds of sand. Records tell that it blew with unabated fury for nine days and nights and when the storm eventually passed, the barony and village of Forvie had vanished—for ever.

Under favourable climatic conditions, Forvie is a region of singular beauty for the subtle play of light and shade on the sweeping sand dunes is constantly changing while the delicate colourings—from the palest grey to the deepest rose —show endless gradations. Of course, when adverse conditions prevail, such as in mist and rain, the area presents a different aspect—a forbidding, eerie picture of desolation and gloom where the chill, disembodied cry of the sea gulls seem fitting accompaniment to Forvie's mournful story.

41

ROYAL ACADEMICIAN

"Art for art's sake."
—Victor Cousin.

THE city of Aberdeen has produced relatively few great artists. This is perhaps natural for, despite the fact that it is a University town and at one period in its history possessed two, Aberdeen is fundamentally a commercial city largely indifferent to the arts.

It is no surprise, therefore, to find that the few great artists cradled in Aberdeen all left the city early in their careers thus escaping the narrow confines of a community where mediocrity has always been appraised and genius ever suspect. Such men as George Jamesone, William Dyce, William Brodie, John Philip and Robert Brough all rose to international fame—but furth their native city.

Of this unusually talented group, William Dyce is doubtless the most remarkable. He was one of those men of genius who might easily have gained distinction in any one of several professions—in medicine, theology, law, science, music or in art—but fortunately for posterity, art was his strongest urge.

Born in the year 1806, William Dyce's roots lay deep in Scotland's north-east corner. As far back as the 15th century, the names of John and Ranald de Dise, both burgesses of Aberdeen, are noted in the city's records, while two other members of the family, Alexander and Brian, are included in the roll of chaplains serving the town's kirk of St. Nicholas. From this family, descended the Dyces of Belhelvie, Cuttlehill, Raeden and Tilliegreig, all in Aberdeenshire.

The main branch of the Dyce family was Belhelvie which originated with William, born in the year 1560. This William Dyce had a son, also called William, and he had two sons, Andrew and Alexander. From the former descended the Dyces of Disblair, Raeden and Tilliegreig, and from the latter the Cuttlehill family originated.

Robert Dyce, 1st of Cuttlehill, was the son of James Dyce, Belhelvie, by his wife Christian Chesser. Robert, who was born in 1729, married his cousin Mary, daughter of Alexander Dyce of Raeden, by whom he had six sons and three daughters In 1777, he acquired Cuttlehill, a property included in the city's Freedom Lands of Sheddocksley about three-and-a-half miles west from Aberdeen. The name Cuttlehill is unknown today for it was changed to Newpark which lies at the western end of the well-known Lang Stracht now part of the city.

Robert Dyce was succeeded at Cuttlehill by his eldest son William (born in 1770) who married Margaret, daughter of James Chalmers of Westburn, by his wife Margaret, daughter and heiress of David Douglas of Tilquhillie in Kincardineshire. William Dyce, 2nd of Cuttlehill, was a prominent physician in Aberdeen where he lived at No. 48 Marischal Street. In this house—built for Dr. Dyce by William (''Sink'em'') Smith, ''meason and vricht'', first of the line of famous Aberdeen architects—several of his family of six sons were born, among them William the future Academician.

William Dyce, artist, was Dr. William's third son. He was born into an unusually talented family, fortunately endowed and in more than comfortable circumstances. Along with his five brothers, William attended Aberdeen Grammar School from which he eventually passed to Marischal College. Here, at the age of sixteen, he graduated M.A. and it was assumed he would study for either the ministry or medicine according to the Dyce family tradition. However, William Dyce's predilection being for art, the youth, already conscious of the north-east's attitude towards this form of expression, worked at his painting in secret. Despite his lack of training, the standard of William's work was high and he found a market for his pictures some of which, belonging to this early period, are still occasionally found in Aberdeen salerooms.

By the time William Dyce was seventeen, he had saved sufficient money from his "secret profession" to enable him to buy a passage on a fishing smack bound for London. Thus, with high hopes, some examples of his work, and a letter of introduction to Sir Thomas Lawrence, President of the Royal Academy, young Dyce took the first important step in his career. He certainly acted up to his family's motto—*"Decide and Dare"*.

Sir Thomas Lawrence was much impressed by Dyce's work. He interceded on the young man's behalf and eventually the douce Aberdeen doctor agreed to his son remaining in London to study art. William began by making drawings in the Egyptian Hall at the British Museum and soon was accepted as a Probationer in the Royal Academy Schools. However, when he was nineteen, an opportunity came to travel to Rome in the company of two famous men, Alexander Day (1773-1841), artist and art dealer, and Holwell Carr (1758-1830), art connoisseur. Dyce jumped at the chance for it came at just the right moment—he had become dissatisfied with the Academy's training methods.

Dyce stayed in Rome for nine months, possibly the happiest, most exciting and stimulating months in his whole life. Everything was new, vibrating with colour and sympathetic to study—a complete contrast to the cold, grey city of his birth. He studied Titian and Nicolas Poussin and the influence of their work is seen in many of his paintings.

In 1826, Dyce returned to Aberdeen. Here he began work on his first important picture, exhibited the following year. At this time, he painted the picture of his mother's home "Westburn", eventually bequeathed to Aberdeen Art Gallery by Dyce's kinsman D. M. A. Chalmers of the Westburn family. More of topographical interest than of artistic value, "Westburn" is important in that the artist took his viewpoint from the neighbouring property of Raeden which belonged to a branch of the Dyce family. During this visit to Aberdeen, Dyce also decorated a room in the Marischal Street home—his first fresco among the many to follow—and perhaps one day, below layers of wallpaper and paint, this early work by the master-hand will be discovered.

From this time onwards, William Dyce's career may be followed in detail in the pages of most standard works on British art.

At the age of twenty-four, he left Aberdeen never to return except for brief visits to his family. He first settled in Edinburgh where in seven years he completed upwards of a hundred portraits, most of them of ministers. This accomplishment gained for him the family name—"William, painter of parsons". Dyce next moved to London, interesting himself in art education and travelling abroad to study teaching methods in other countries. In 1844, he was appointed Professor of Fine Arts at King's College, London, a prelude to his "fresco period" which is now a matter of history. Eventually, Dyce settled in Streatham where he lived with his wife Jane Brand and their family until his death in 1864.

William Dyce possessed many of the finest qualities of the Scottish race—energy, industry, tenacity and skill. He was an unusually keen observer of nature, a restless spirit, perhaps, while his approach to art was detached and precise, that of a cultured mind rather than of a Bohemian. Dyce's contribution to British Art and in particular to Art Education is only now being appreciated— over a century after his death.

Facing.   1. Parish Church, Crimond.
2. Tillyfruskie Ha'-house.

1

2

PLATE 22

42

WHO REALLY COMPOSED "CRIMOND"?

"The Church with psalms must shout,
No door can keep them out;
But above all, the heart
Must bear the longest part."

—George Herbert.

THE current edition of *The Scottish Psalter* issued by the joint authority of the General Assemblies of the Church of Scotland and the United Free Church, states that the psalm tune No. 47—*Crimond*—is the composition of Jessie Seymour Irvine (1836-1889). The name of David Grant (1833-1893), which had consistently appeared as the composer of *Crimond* for upwards of eighty years, has been deleted and in consequence passes from the annals of Scottish psalmody. No explanation is given and this is not surprising.

Crimond is surely one of the most popular tunes in *The Scottish Psalter* for, wedded to the words of the 23rd Psalm, it has been sung with deep feeling on a great many important occasions. It is often assumed that *Crimond* is one of our older Scottish psalm tunes and that it was composed specially to the words of the 23rd Psalm. Actually, neither assumption is correct for *Crimond* is a comparatively recent composition and was originally set to the words of a hymn by George Washington Doane (1799-1859).

Facing. Lochnager—1854.

N

Before the advent of *Crimond*, the 23rd Psalm was most frequently sung to the tune *Kilmarnock*, the composition of Neil Dougall (1766-1862) of Greenock. But fashions change —even in church music—and so today, the 23rd Psalm is most often sung to the tune *Crimond*.

The 23rd Psalm has been called "Scotland's Psalm" on account of the fact that, wherever Scots people gather for worship, it is sung with verve "for every line of it, every word of it has been engraven for generations on Scottish hearts, has accompanied them from childhood to age, from their homes to all the seas and lands where they have wandered".

Thus, largely through its close association with the 23rd Psalm, the tune *Crimond* has become world-famous. In 1947, the inclusion of *Crimond* in the Order of Service at the marriage of Her Majesty The Queen to H.R.H. Prince Philip, Duke of Edinburgh, increased its popularity, while the beautiful recording of *Crimond* made by Sir Hugh Roberton and the Glasgow Orpheus Choir gave it to the public at large.

The tune *Crimond* takes its name from Crimond in Aberdeenshire which lies at the extreme north-east corner of Scotland. It is a flat, rather bare countryside, but is not without charm. The village of Crimond is about midway between Peterhead and Fraserburgh, and here, on the roadside, stands the parish church which has become so closely identified with the popular psalm tune. It was during the ministry at Crimond of the Rev. Alexander Irvine, D.D. (1805-1884) that the psalm tune *Crimond* was composed.

In the month of March, 1855, the Rev. Alexander Irvine, formerly of Dunnottar in Kincardineshire, was translated at his own request from Peterhead to Crimond. Here he remained as parish minister until his death in 1884. By his wife Jessie Nicol, he had a family of eight, five sons and three daughters, the second daughter being Jessie Seymour Irvine.

Jessie Seymour Irvine was musically inclined and sang in the choir of Crimond Church, then under the leadership of

William Clubb, precentor. William Clubb (1855-1915), was saddler in the village of Crimond. He was an able precentor, had a profound knowledge of Scottish psalmody and was famed far beyond the bounds of the parish of Crimond. He was therefore cognisant of everything appertaining to the praise in Crimond Church—an important point in the *Crimond* story.

Towards the middle of last century, a remarkable wave of interest in church music swept over Scotland. Nowhere was this more manifest than in the north-east where a small band of enthusiasts, headed by William Carnie (1824-1908), journalist and precentor in Aberdeen, was collaborating in collecting and collating everything they could find relating to Scottish psalmody.

This musical coterie included Robert Cooper (1841-1905), precentor in Peterhead and later in Aberdeen; the already mentioned William Clubb (1855-1915), precentor in Crimond; and David Grant (1833-1893), composer, Aberdeen. Two other musical friends were often consulted—John Johnstone, precentor, Old Deer, and David Taylor, soloist, Aberdeen.

In 1859, William Carnie commenced publishing psalm tunes—old and new—in four-paged, penny "Fly Leaves". As these accumulated with the passing years, and as they had proved to be extremely popular, Carnie decided to publish them in book form so *The Northern Psalter* appeared in 1872.

In his preface to the 1st Edition of the *Psalter*, William Carnie mentions "four original tunes" (viz.: tunes which had not already appeared in his "Fly Leaves") and one of them is tune No. 109—*Crimond* by David Grant. In his index, Carnie gives the name of David Grant as being the composer of two tunes—*Raleigh* (composed in 1867) and *Crimond* (composed in 1871) and says that both of these tunes by Grant were harmonised by him specially for *The Northern Psalter*.

Before William Carnie died in 1908, more than seventy thousand copies of *The Northern Psalter* had been sold and up to that date—a period of thirty-six years—nobody had questioned the accuracy of the statements contained therein. This was confirmed by Carnie's grandson in September, 1924.

David Grant (1833-1893), whom William Carnie stated was the composer of *Raleigh* and *Crimond*, was born in Aberdeen on 19th September, 1833. Little is known of his early life except that he received his education in one of the city's schools and served his apprenticeship with John Duncan, tobacconist in Aberdeen. In 1853, at the early age of twenty, David Grant succeeded to Duncan's business and with the passing years prospered. Eventually Grant had the honour of becoming a Royal Warrant Holder to Queen Victoria.

However, David Grant's real interest was in music. He studied under Herr Granz and became a first-class, all-round musician-composer, soloist and instrumentalist. He was a life-long member of Fittie Kirk (now East St. Clements) where he sang in the choir. He was known to a very wide circle in the north-east and was one of William Carnie's closest friends. In 1878, David Grant retired from business and went to live in London. As far as is known, he never returned to his native city and died at his home *"Bon-Accord"* in Forest Hill, London, on 30th July, 1893.

Grant was the composer of several psalm tunes but, apart from *Raleigh* and *Crimond* attributed to him by Carnie, nothing appears to have survived. It is said that Grant dedicated the tune *Raleigh* to the "founder" of the tobacco trade, while *Crimond* was dedicated to his many friends in Crimond including William Clubb, the precentor, and the Irvines at the manse. David Grant lies in an unmarked grave in Ladywell Cemetery, London.

In 1911, eighteen years after David Grant's death and three years after the death of William Carnie, the first "whisperings" were heard in the north-east that David Grant was not the composer of *Crimond* and that William Carnie had surreptitiously given credit to his friend where credit was not due. This arose when the then minister of Crimond received a letter dated 31st May, 1911, from Anna Barbara Irvine (1830-1924) stating that her late sister, Jessie Seymour

Irvine, was the composer of *Crimond* and she thought that William Carnie had got David Grant to harmonise it. This letter—now in the Library at King's College, Old Aberdeen —was immediately accepted as ''proof'' that Jessie Seymour Irvine was the composer of *Crimond*, yet the ''documentary evidence'' as it has been called, would never be accepted as proof by any Court of Law.

At this point, two people with first-hand knowledge of the matter made strong protest—William Clubb, the old precentor at Crimond, and George Riddell, Rosehearty, both of whom had been associated with William Carnie in the preparation of *The Northern Psalter*. They pointed out that Anna Barbara Irvine—then in her 82nd year—had confounded the tune *Crimond*, which they confirmed had been composed by David Grant, with a tune called *Ballantyne* composed by Jessie Seymour Irvine and harmonised for her by David Grant. There had been a sad and painful chapter in the life of Jessie Seymour Irvine and the tune *Ballantyne* was associated with it.

At this time, however, there was one other person with first-hand information regarding *Crimond*—and still living in the neighbourhood. This was Jessie Seymour Irvine's brother Patrick Irvine (1832-1918), solicitor, Peterhead. He made no comment, which is significant.

The testimonies of both William Clubb and George Riddell were summarily brushed aside and the cry went up for justice to be done to Jessie Seymour Irvine, implying, of course, that sometime in the past an ''injustice'' had been committed. But by whom?

The years passed and now David Grant's name has been deleted from *The Scottish Psalter* but whether those who clamoured for ''justice'' have themselves acted justly is quite another matter.

43

TILLIEFRUSKIE'S HA'

"Every spirit makes its house; but afterwards
the house confines the spirit."
—Emerson.

ALTHOUGH the county of Aberdeen is justly famous for the remarkable number of castellated buildings within its boundaries, it is equally rich in lesser structures, the simple "ha'-houses"—hall-like-houses—of the 17th and 18th centuries. Unlike their more elaborate predecessors, these quaint old buildings have been rather neglected yet they are a fruitful field of study as, apart from their architectural interest, most of them possess histories every bit as romantic as those of their more spectacular and more widely publicised elders.

Despite the fact that the past fifty years have witnessed the demolition of some noteworthy examples, quite a number of fine old "ha'houses" have escaped destruction and with present-day legislation, would appear to stand a reasonable chance of survival to enrich posterity.

One of the most fascinating of these houses is the little-known Ha' of Tillyfruskie on Feughside. It occupies a fine, open situation on the left bank of the Feugh Water—a tributary of the River Dee—about midway between Whitestone and Finzean. The name Tillyfruskie is of Gaelic origin —from the words *tulach chrasgaidh* "knoll of the crossing", which doubtless refers to the nearby crossing over the well-known Corsedardar Hill.

182

The lands of Tillyfruskie are first mentioned in the year 1170. At that date, they were included in the Royal Forest of Birse which in 1242 was gifted by Alexander II (1214-1249) to Ralph, Bishop of Aberdeen. Thereafter, until the Reformation in 1560, the Forest of Birse remained church property. In 1556, William, Bishop of Aberdeen, granted the lands of Tillyfruskie "lyand within his baronie of Birse" to Andrew Strachan and his wife Christian Sibbald, and at Stirling in 1586, confirmation of this grant was made by James VI (1567-1625).

Andrew Strachan appears to have had a family of three sons and a daughter—Alexander, heir to Tillyfruskie; William of Cluny; John, Rector of Kincardine, who married Agnes co-heiress of Andrew Hunter, burgess of Aberdeen; and Margaret, wife of James Gordon of Drumgask. In 1597 and with the consent of Alexander his heir, Andrew Strachan transferred Tillyfruskie to his wife's kinsman John Sibbald, younger of Keir. Eventually, Sibbald disposed of the property to John Irvine of Kinnoch but in 1601 Tillyfruskie was again acquired by the Strachans—by the already-mentioned William of Cluny. William Strachan married Christian, daughter of Archibald Irvine of Whitestone, a neighbouring property, which their third son William subsequently inherited from his maternal grandfather. A curiously phrased document of the period tells that Irvine of Whitestone was "bound in 500 merks that Tillyfruskie would not slay salmon in the forbidden time with any kind of engine."

By the year 1638, Tillyfruskie had passed from the Strachans to Robert Garden of Boghead, the adjacent property, whose son Gilbert inherited Tillyfruskie *circa* 1645. Gilbert Garden became an ardent "Brownist" and shortly after joining this movement, the parish minister reports to the Deeside Presbytery that "Tillyfruskie has dishantit (forsaken) the kirk" of Birse for which "crime" Gilbert was excommunicated. Gilbert Garden was succeeded by his son John who, about the year 1690, disposed of Tillyfruskie to James Ochterlony described in the Poll Book of 1696 as being "married, with four children".

The Ochterlonys of Tillyfruskie are believed to have stemmed from the Ochterlonys of that ilk in Angus, the Ochterlonys of the Guynd being the most noted branch of the family. Of James Ochterlony, 1st of Tillyfruskie, little is known except that he was succeeded by his son David who recorded arms in the Lyon Court. In 1731, he obtained a charter of the lands of Learney, near Torphins, but in 1736 transferred this property to his son Peter who in 1707 had married Margaret Buchan, fifth daughter of Major James Buchan of Auchmacoy and his wife Mary, daughter of Sir John Forbes, 2nd Baronet of Craigievar—the "Red Sir John" of local legends. Margaret Buchan, the widow of John Ramsay of Barra and Laithers, would seem to have been the first wife of Peter Ochterlony for the initials displayed on the Ha' of Tillyfruskie—which he built—are not those of Margaret Buchan but "I. F." with the date 1733 which suggests that either this was the year in which Peter married for a second time, or it was the date when he built the house. At all events, the identity of "I. F." remains obscure. In 1747, Peter Ochterlony conveyed Learney to his brother-in-law William Brebner who had married Major James Buchan's fourth daughter Jane.

In addition to Peter, his heir, David Ochterlony had three daughters and a son—Elizabeth who married Francis Douglas, author and publisher; Bathia, the wife of Charles Tait, Sheriff-Substitute of Aberdeenshire; Mary, who married Alexander Dyce and who died in Aberdeen in 1826 at the advanced age of 95; and Captain David Ochterlony, killed at Quebec in 1759. Peter was the last Ochterlony laird of Tillyfruskie which subsequently merged with the other Farquharson properties forming the estate of Finzean.

The name of Captain David Ochterlony of Tillyfruskie forms an interesting link between the north-east of Scotland and the struggle for Canada. Although some years younger than General James Wolfe, David formed a friendship with the hero of Quebec; indeed Ochterlony appears to have been the only Scotsman for whom Wolfe had any respect. When the two men first met is uncertain but it must have been either during the Jacobite Rising of 1745—Wolfe had obtained his Captaincy in 1744 at the age of 17—or when he was on garrison duty in Scotland for various periods from 1749 to 1757. During the '45 Wolfe was with the Duke of Cumberland in Aberdeen and it is possible he met Ochterlony at this time. At the age of 16, Wolfe had distinguished himself at the battle of Dettingen and at the age of 18 may well have inspired young Ochterlony to embark on a military career. Whether or not General Wolfe ever visited Tillyfruskie is doubtful but by no means impossible.

At all events, David Ochterlony, a Captain commanding a detachment of the 60th King's Royal Rifle Corps, was in the landing-party alongisde General Wolfe when the assault on Quebec began on the morning of 31st July, 1759. The previous night, Ochterlony had fought a duel with a brother-officer Captain Wetterstroom, a German serving with the Grenadiers. Ochterlony was wounded, but next morning took his place in the landing-craft and under exceptionally heavy fire from the French sharpshooters strategically placed above them on the Plains of Abraham, was successful in landing his detachment on the strand below. He then led his party up the rocky terrain and in the assault was severely wounded. During a lull in the battle, a party of Red Indians attempted to scalp him where he lay but were driven off by a young officer, Lieut. Henry Payton, who himself was wounded. The Red Indians again attacked, stabbing Ochterlony in the stomach with their scalping knives. However, he continued to fight back while the Indians tried to strangle him with his sash. For a second time, the Indians were driven off. David Ochterlony was then carried from the field to the General Hospital in Quebec where he died shortly after admission. His friend General Wolfe was fatally wounded in the hour of victory. The General's body was brought home and buried in Greenwich Church, but David Ochterlony was laid to rest in Quebec far from his native Tillyfruskie.

For three generations, the Ochterlonys continued at Tillyfruskie which remains virtually the same as it did in their time.
The old Ha' of **1733** consists of a simple, well-proportioned,
rectangular building of two storeys and a garret—a "laigh-
biggin' " was added sometime later—and it possesses all the
refinements of the period. The whole atmosphere of Tillyfruskie is redolent of the 18th century and it is refreshing to
find extant so fine and complete an example.

44

PHOTOGRAPHER ROYAL

"Nature I loved, and, next to Nature, Art."
    —W. S. Landor.

IN the year 1860, a new appointment was made to Queen Victoria's household—that of *Photographer Royal to Her Majesty in Scotland*. It was a startling innovation for the camera was still in its infancy. Some years earlier, during his travels in upper Deeside, a young and enthusiastic photographer had taken a picture of Balmoral Castle—a unique topographical record as it happened, for the old castle's days were numbered. It was an excellent picture and greatly pleased the Queen who was deeply attached to the place. Accordingly, in 1855, the photographer received a Royal command to come to old Balmoral Castle for the purpose of "taking likenesses of Her Majesty and the Royal Family"— then considered to be a somewhat "daring" experiment. The cameraman was G. W. Wilson of Aberdeen, Scotland's pioneer photographer.

Over a century has elapsed since G. W. Wilson took his "likenesses" at Balmoral—actually the first occasion on which a reigning Sovereign and her family had submitted to the "ordeal" of this new form of art. In that time, few professions have undergone such revolutionary changes, for in the early days of photography—as indeed in every other occupation—there was no easy way. G. W. Wilson started from scratch. He studied and worked very hard at this new and fascinating medium and in forty years succeeded in building up for himself an international reputation as a photographer.

George Washington Wilson was born at Waulkmill of Carnousie in the parish of Forglen, Banffshire, in 1823. He was the second son of George Wilson (1777-1848), Culvie, in the parish of Marnoch, Banffshire, and his wife Elizabeth Herd, Turriff, Aberdeenshire. This George Wilson had a remarkable career which demands a word. At the age of sixteen, he embarked on a fishing smack at Banff bound for Edinburgh where he intended doing some business for his father. However, on arrival at Leith, the vessel was boarded by a Press-gang seeking young men for the Napoleonic Wars, and George Wilson was immediately seized. Twenty-four years were to elapse before he returned to his native Banffshire. He saw much active service in Hanover, the Netherlands and in the Peninsular War where he served under the Duke of Wellington. By this time, George Wilson had risen to the rank of Sergeant-Major. He then volunteered for service in Canada but two years later returned to Scotland settling in Banffshire where he farmed the holding of Waulk-mill of Carnousie. Wilson had married "on the strength" while in Portugal but his wife and three children were drowned when the ship bringing them to Scotland foundered in the Bay of Biscay. George Wilson's second wife was the already mentioned Elizabeth Herd by whom he had a family of eleven. He died in 1848 and lies in the remote kirkyard at Alvah in Banffshire.

George Washington Wilson's upbringing was similar to that of many another country "loon" of the time. Whenever he was old enough to help on the farm, his father set him to clear the land of stones—hard and tedious work for a young boy—but in later life, when visiting Waulkmill, he would look with pride on the lush fields cleared by his brothers and himself in their youth. G. W. Wilson attended Forglen School, two miles from his home, where he showed an apti-tude for drawing and working with his hands. Opportunities for employment were few in Banffshire and so, at the age of twelve, he was apprenticed to the local joiner. However, his sojourn in carpentry and joinery lasted only during the term of his apprenticeship for young Wilson was determined to make art his career.   During his employment with the local joiner, Wilson's time had not been wasted for he became familiar with beautiful things such as the different styles of furniture sent for repair and the various collections of pictures in the great houses where he worked—Carnousie, Forglen, Cullen and Duff House, the last-named the seat of the Earls of Fife.

Having inherited something of his father's adventurous spirit, he set off for Edinburgh where he studied art at the Academy Schools.   Here he made considerable progress and eventually moved to London where he entered the Royal Academy School.   Although Wilson enjoyed landscape painting, his real interest lay in portraiture, especially in miniatures. This highly specialised form of painting was then extremely popular and Wilson studied under the best teachers including Henry Corbould of London.   He also studied for a time in Paris.

In 1848, G. W. Wilson returned to Scotland settling in Aberdeen where he went into partnership with John Hay, carver and gilder (later Messrs. Hay & Lyall).   This partnership, although of short duration, was a happy one. Eventually, Wilson set up on his own account teaching drawing and painting and carrying out his many commissions in portraiture—usually of kitcat size or miniatures.   At this time, Wilson's friends included James Giles (1801-1870), William Dyce (1806-1864), Alexander Brodie (1815-1881) the sculptor, John Philip (1817-1867) and James Cassie (1801-1870).

He paid a short visit to London in 1849 and this trip proved to be the turning point in his remarkable career.   In London, he saw some calotypes made by Fox Talbot "likenesses of sitters produced by the chemical reaction of sunlight on sensitised surfaces".   Excellent "likenesses" they were, all produced without any manual work.   Wilson was much impressed.   He was also rudely shaken for he realised that, should this new method of obtaining "likenesses" prove popular, his days as a miniature portrait painter would soon be over.   Back in Aberdeen, Wilson immediately set about studying chemistry and optics. He then built himself a camera—a rather primitive affair—but it served. Thereafter, Wilson spent all his spare time experimenting.

In 1849, George Washington Wilson married Maria Ann Cassie (1827-1912), grand-daughter of James Cruickshank, farmer, Balquhain, Aberdeenshire, who belonged to the old Quaker line from which derived Amos and Anthony Cruickshank of Sittyton, the world-famous cattle breeders (see Chapter 34). The couple had a family of ten—six sons and four daughters.

Despite his growing interest in photography, G. W. Wilson never entirely gave up drawing and painting and right to the end of his life always carried a sketch-book in his pocket. Consequently, it was in 1850 that one of his most important contributions to the topographical records of Aberdeen was made—*A Delineation of the City*. This was a panoramic bird's-eye view of Aberdeen and entailed a fantastic amount of work for every building portrayed is drawn in detail. The *Delineation* was lithographed by Messrs. Keith & Gibb of Aberdeen and copies of this unusual drawing are now quite rare.

Like most photographers, Wilson's first attempts in the medium were of his family and his friends but soon he was taking landscapes—chiefly of Deeside. Today, of course, such photographic pilgrimages are simple matters but in Wilson's time they were major operations as his log-books show. His first "quick-exposure" was taken in 1856—Princes Street, Edinburgh, and this along with his H.M.S. *Cambridge* at Great Gun Practice, created a sensation when they were exhibited in London. By this time, Wilson had trained a staff of photographers which enabled him to move about the country in search of subjects—landscapes and places of historic interest—for he had developed a most lucrative business in the production of stereoscopic views and picture post-cards. On his staff at Aberdeen were two London men—Geering and Fry—the latter to become a partner in the well-known photographic business Messrs. Elliot & Fry. The difficulties encountered by Wilson on his earlier trips to the Highlands of Scotland are almost beyond belief for there were no railways or motor cars and the roads were very poor— sometimes mere tracks. This was long before the days of miniature cameras and all the bulky photographic equipment had to be carried in hampers by Wilson and his assistants. A great step forward was made when he designed and had constructed a special horse-drawn van—a travelling dark- room with sink, cistern, shelves, etc.—and in this peripatetic studio, G. W. Wilson travelled the length and breadth of Great Britain.

In 1860, George Washington Wilson was honoured by Queen Victoria when he received the appointment of *Photographer Royal to Her Majesty in Scotland*. It was a well-deserved honour. He was then commissioned to make a complete set of photographs of Balmoral Castle, Windsor Castle and other Royal residences. It is no exaggeration to say that every one of these pictures is a masterpiece of the photographer's art. Climatic conditions seldom worry the professional photographer today, but in Wilson's time they were frequently the deciding factor. It was due to adverse weather conditions that G. W. Wilson had to abandon what might well have been the highlight of his professional career. On several occasions, Wilson had taken "likenesses" of Prince Frederick William of Prussia at Balmoral, and now in 1871, the Prince's father William I was to be crowned Emperor of Germany so had appointed Wilson to cover the ceremony. Much to Wilson's regret, the climatic conditions were against him and the project had to be abandoned.

There is no doubt that much of Wilson's success as a photographer was due to the fact that he was, first and last, an artist. His compositions—whether in landscape, architecture, portraiture or groups—all show the artist's feeling for massing and line. This, together with the excellence of his technical achievements at a time when every piece of photographic equipment had to be made by the photographer himself, singles "G.W.W." out from amongst all the other early exponents of the art.

It is only now that George Washington Wilson's place in Scotland is being fully recognised. His valuable work as a topographical photographer cannot be overestimated for he has left to posterity a fantastic amount of material on the countryside, the coast, the historic buildings and places of interest, the towns and villages, the industries, the people and their way of life over a century ago.

When Wilson died in Aberdeen in 1893, it was said that while the public discovered Scotland through the pen of Sir Walter Scott, it was equally certain that they had become familiar with Scotland through the camera of George Washington Wilson.

PLATE 24

45

AT THE CROSSROADS OF HISTORY

"Truth is strength."
—Motto of Kintore.

IN these days of constant change, it is refreshing to come across an instance of continuity—of a living society where man has remained and held the same set of values for upwards of a thousand years. This is not the story of a great city with a teeming population and multiple resources but the simple tale of a modest Aberdeenshire village, a centre of rural life, the history of which is lost in the mists of antiquity—the Royal burgh of Kintore.

Kintore stands on the right bank of the River Don about twelve miles north-west from Aberdeen and four miles south-east from Inverurie. Located within the parish of the same name, Kintore is picturesquely situated on one of the many "loops" of the slow-moving Don as it meanders through the historic Lordship of the Garioch.

That Kintore was early an important centre is clear from the prehistoric remains found there. Bronze Age hill-forts, cattle-camps and stone circles are the tangible evidence of an ancient civilisation while the Kintore sculptured stones—two of which are in the National Museum of Antiquities, Edinburgh—prove that a high level of culture existed here in the remote past.

It is an established fact that Kintore was a place of importance in Roman times for, west from the village, is the

Facing. Loch Muick and the Glas-allt Shiel.

o

site of a Roman marching-camp. This camp was one of a chain in the Roman route north and is believed to have been occupied by the legions of Septimius Severus probably between the years 208-211 A.D.

Tradition tells that Kintore's first charter was granted by King Kenneth II (971-995)—possibly a "word of mouth" grant. During a struggle against the Danes, the villagers of Kintore turned out for the king, bringing their cattle with them. Camouflaged with oak branches, the cattle were stampeded through the enemy lines creating such havoc that King Kenneth won the day. In gratitude, he created Kintore a Royal burgh. The earliest extant charter, however, is dated 3rd February, 1506, and was granted to Kintore by James IV (1488-1513).

By the 13th century, the history of Kintore becomes more definite. It was then the centre of the Royal Forest of Kintore—a hunting forest of the early Scottish kings. Here, hard by the church, the king erected a stronghold, a motte-and-bailey castle of earthwork and timber, and it was there in 1273 that Alexander III (1249-1286) granted his charter to the burgesses of Aberdeen. Nothing of the castle survives for the castle-hill was removed to make way for the railway line. One of the most famous visitors to Kintore Castle was Edward I of England—the "Hammer of the Scots"—who halted there in the summer of 1296 on his progress north from Aberdeen to Elgin.

During the War of Succession and Independence, Kintore again came to prominence for Robert the Bruce (1306-1329) was frequently in the district. Not far from the village are "Bruce's Camp" where the king's army lay the night before the battle of Barra (1308), and "Bruce's Cave" where the king sheltered and where—as local legend has it—he encountered the famous spider. It is not surprising, therefore, to find that in 1309, the Forest of Kintore—with the exception of the king's castle and park—was granted by Bruce to Sir Robert Keith, Great Marischal of Scotland. The grant was made in recognition of Sir Robert's services to the Royal cause for the king had not forgotten Keith's heroic cavalry charge against the English bowmen at Bannockburn which contributed in no small measure to victory. Soon after the grant was made, Hallforest Castle was built as the capital messuage of the Royal Forest. It is a typical 14th century keep-tower and, despite its ruinous condition, is an impressive landmark in the Kintore district. The castle was abandoned and fell into decay on the erection of Keith Hall in 1665.

As one would expect in such an ancient community, several of the burgh's feus were held direct from the Crown. One of these was the Goose Croft—from the Gaelic *guibhais* meaning "fir-wood"—which is believed to have been granted by King James II (1437-1460), and this seems likely for in 17th century records, the Goose Croft is referred to as "the King's gift".

Thus, all down the centuries, Kintore has played its part in Scottish history. For example in the Trials for Witchcraft of 1596, Isobel Cockie in Kintore was condemned to be "brint at ye staiks" and the accounts for the materials necessary for the carrying out of this terrible sentence are still preserved. In Covenanting times and during the Jacobite Rising of 1745, Kintore figured prominently for its situation on the main north route made it a key point as indeed it had been since Roman times.

By far the most fascinating building in Kintore today is the Town House and Tolbooth. It is a remarkably fine piece of Scottish architecture and it is to Kintore's lasting credit that they appreciate its merit and preserve it with care. The building was erected between the years 1737 and 1747, the gift of John Keith, 3rd Earl of Kintore. The Town House stands on the historic market place of the burgh where, for many centuries, the famous Mary Mass Fair was held annually. It is appropriate that in Kintore's heraldic bearings, due consideration is given to its ancient traditions for they display the cattle and the oak branches associated with King Kenneth II in his victory over the Danes—and of course the motto which links it with the Earl Marischal's family *"Truth is strength"*.

46

THE WIDOW'S HOUSE

"Land of brown heath and shaggy wood,
Land of the mountain and the flood."
—Sir Walter Scott.

OF all the Royal residences in Great Britain, the Glas-allt Shiel on the Balmoral Estate is one of the most fascinating. Starkly dominated by great, heather-clad mountains scored by deep-cut ravines, the shiel is perfectly situated on the western shores of Loch Muick. At 1,313 feet above sea-level, the awsome grandeur of its setting is breath-taking.

Loch Muick occupies the upper part of a narrow glen of the same name. Situated at the south-east corner of the Balmoral Estate, it is the largest sheet of water on Deeside, being over two miles in length with an average breadth of a third of a mile. Lying mostly on a flat-bottomed rock basin, the surface of the loch covers an area of around 550 acres and in places has a depth of over 256 feet.

Glen Muick has an interesting history. Its name derives from the Gaelic word *muc* meaning "pig"—the "pig's glen" —suggesting its former use as a summer pasturage. In the remote past, the area was included in the extensive Celtic Province of Mar whose Mormaers, or Chiefs, are on record from the year 1014. During the 12th century, the Mormaers of Mar adopted the Normanising policy of the Royal House of Dunkeld. Consequently, the Celtic Province gradually developed into a feudal Earldom. Sometime during the 13th century, the Earls of Mar settled the Scoto-Norman family of

Bisset on Deeside and Glen Muick was included in their grant of land. In due course, the Bissets were succeeded by the Frasers who in turn were followed by the Keiths, Great Marischals of Scotland. About the middle of the 15th century, Glen Muick was acquired by the Gordons, Earls of Huntly, who in 1749 disposed of the eastern section of the glen to the Farquharsons of Invercauld. However, in 1863, this portion was sold by the Farquharsons to Sir James Mackenzie, Bt., who assumed the territorial title "of Glenmuick". The western section of the glen—which includes Birkhall, the Deeside residence of H.M. Queen Elizabeth, The Queen Mother—was eventually acquired by H.R.H. Prince Albert.

Queen Victoria first came to Deeside in September, 1848. Her visit was brief, lasting barely three weeks, but it was long enough for the Queen and her Consort to lose their hearts to the valley and they returned the following year. They came again in 1850 and 1851. Then in 1852, Prince Albert purchased the Balmoral Estate and gifted it to the Queen.

From her *Journal of Our Life in the Highlands*, it appears Queen Victoria first visited Glen Muick in August, 1849, when she and Prince Albert were staying in the bothy at Allt-naguibhsaich—the "burn-of-the-fir-wood"—a tributary of the Muick. During the afternoon, the Royal party sailed up the loch, fishing as they went. The Queen tells that they caught seventy trout before landing on the sandy delta formed by the turbulent Glas-allt—the "grey burn"—which enters the loch from the west. Both Victoria and Albert were quite enchanted by the scene from the delta and it became their favourite picnic spot. That evening, the Queen set down her impressions of the expedition—"the scenery is beautiful, so wild and grand . . . . . I wish an artist could have been there to sketch the scene". As it happened, Queen Victoria herself recorded the scene some twenty years later, in one of her charming watercolour paintings.

At this time, there stood on the Glas-allt delta a small shiel—the old Scots word for a shelter—used by deer-stalkers.

The only overland approach to this isolated shiel was by a narrow, winding bridle-path along the steep, western shores of Loch Muick, but shortly after coming into possession of Balmoral, Prince Albert had this difficult access remade as a carriage road. The deer-stalkers' shiel also received attention. It was re-modelled as a picnic cottage and the Queen tells it contained "a charming room for us, commanding a most lovely view". The first Royal picnic took place here on 16th September, 1852, when Victoria and Albert enjoyed "the cold luncheon" brought with them. After the meal, the party ascended the arduous Glas-allt path to the Dubh Loch—a climb of 800 feet in less than two miles. Delighted with the wild and rugged scenery, the Queen sat down to sketch but had only just begun when one of her ghillies arrived with official dispatches from Balmoral—a "service" which of necessity had to follow Her Majesty even to the most remote corners of the Highlands. Alas! one of the letters brought sad news—the death of the great and much-loved Duke of Wellington—so the happy expedition was brought to a sorrowful conclusion and the party returned to the shiel.

In the following years, the shiel was frequently visited by Victoria and her Consort. But the year 1861 brought tragedy —the death of Prince Albert—so the shiel, rich in happy memories, thereafter became a place of pilgrimage for the surviving partner—

> *"Where love has been, there yet remains*
> *an echo of the song that once it sung".*

These pilgrimages continued annually until 1867 when the Queen decided to erect a new Glas-allt Shiel on the delta. As she writes in her *Journal*, Albert "always wished to build here, in this favourite wild spot, quite in amidst the hills".

The task of planning the shiel—the third to occupy the picturesque site—fell to John Beaton. He had acted as clerk-of-works during the building of Balmoral Castle and on its completion was appointed resident architect on the Balmoral

Estate. Of course Beaton was by this time familiar with Prince Albert's ideas and taste in architecture, and the new shiel was designed in keeping with other buildings on the estate erected during the Prince's lifetime. It was modestly proportioned, but as the Queen records had a ''wonderful deal of room'' in it. The principal apartments—the Queen's sitting-room, dining-room and bedroom—faced Loch Muick.

The ''house-warming'' at the Glas-allt Shiel took place on Thursday evening, 1st October, 1868. The ''ceremony'' is graphically described by the Queen in her *Journal*—a lively evening with ''whisky-toddy'' to toast the ''fire-kindling''. Five animated Highland reels brought the ''house-warming'' party to a close although, as the Queen recounts with commendable tact, ''the men went on singing in the steward's room for some time, and all were very happy''.

Later that evening, the Queen writes—''Sad thoughts filled my heart . . . . . the happy past and my darling husband whom I fancied I must see . . . . . a sad though struck me . . . . . a 'Widow's House', not built by him or hallowed by his memory''.

Thereafter, every year until the end of her lengthy reign, Queen Victoria spent some days at the isolated Glas-allt Shiel, usually in October when early snows capped the great mountains. A true lover of nature, she gathered strength from this rugged countryside.

Over a century passed. The ''Widow's House'' stands unaltered on its sandy delta and after six reigns the only outward signs of change are the pine trees grown to maturity. They were planted by the great Queen.

DESCRIPTION OF THE PLATES

Frontispiece.

This fascinating "delineation" of Aberdeen was made by James Gordon, Parson of Rothiemay, in 1661. His view-point would appear to have been from what is now North Silver Street looking north-eastwards over the "Corbie Heugh"—now Union Terrace Gardens. In the foreground, a group of citizens are shown taking a leisurely stroll on the outskirts of the burgh—probably it is a Friday as one of the female figures drives a well-laden pack-horse towards the Green.

At the extreme left of the picture is the south-west corner of the Loch—the "Loch-e'e" (now Crooked Lane)—while above it is "The Wynde Mill" at the head of the Gallowgate—on the site now covered by the Gallowgate flats. In the centre is the gable of the Blackfriars' Monastery, the Grammar School in Schoolhill, and to the right the spire of Greyfriars Church. The Kirk of St. Nicholas is a prominent feature and to the right of it is the spirelet of the Bede House in Correction Wynd. At the extreme right of the picture is the Tolbooth in the Castlegate.

PLATE 1.

1. Pediment of a dormer window—now built into the gable of a property in the Square at Ellon—showing the armorial bearings of the Forbes family of Waterton who claimed, through their acquiring the lands of Kermuck, the right to display the crossed keys of the hereditary Constables of Aberdeen.

2. Wrought-iron key believed to be that of Aberdeen's Shiprow Port. The similarity in its design to those displayed on the Forbes of Waterton pediment is quite marked. The key is in the Provost Skene House collection.

3. King Robert the Bruce's charter of 1319 is preserved in the Charter Room of the Town House. Its story is given in *City by the grey North Sea*.

PLATE 2.

1. Ruthrieston's Pack Bridge in its original position crossing the Pot Burn. Built of "aistler-wark" in 1693-94, it was removed in 1923 to its present site 34 yards eastwards and rebuilt with parapets which completely destroyed its unique character. Ruadri's gallows stood a short distance west from the bridge.

2. The plaque in Ruthrieston Sports Ground, Pitstruan Place, erected in 1960 to mark the site of old Pitmuxton House

PLATE 3.

1. The photograph is of the original figure of *Our Ladye of Good Success* now preserved in the parish church of Finistere in Brussels.

2. The ruins of St. Fittick's Church, Nigg. The "lepers' squint", now built up, is set in the north wall of the church.

PLATE 4.

1. Bronze fertility charm found in a Shiprow property occupying the southern slopes of St. Catherine's Hill. It is preserved in the Provost Skene's House collection.

2. This portrait of James VI and I by George Jamesone, the Aberdeen artist, is in the private collection of William S. Bell, Esq., antique dealer. It is displayed in an elaborately-carved frame contemporary with the painting and incorporates the Royal arms of the period subsequent to James's succession to the English throne.

3. The Wallace Tower in the Nether Kirkgate, Aberdeen, as it appeared a century ago. The photograph is by George Washington Wilson.

PLATE 5.

1. This photograph of George Jamesone's House in Schoolhill is also by George Washington Wilson. It was taken shortly before the property was demolished in 1886.

2. Portrait of Brother Francis, the murdered Red Friar, now in the ancient church of Palma on the island of Majorca. Said to be of Spanish workmanship, the artist is unknown.

PLATE 6.

1. The Well o' Spa in Spa Street is now the only reminder of George Jamesone's "Four Neykit Gardyn", later called "The Playe Field", where Shakespeare may have acted in 1601.

2. The dried and mummified right arm, said to be that of the Marquis of Montrose, which was exhibited to the Society of Antiquaries of Scotland in 1896.

3. Montrose's letter to the Provost and Magistrates of Aberdeen written on 13th September, 1644, from his camp at the "Twa-mile-Cross", near Aberdeen. The story of the sacking of Aberdeen is given in *City by the grey North Sea*. Montrose's Deeside campaign is given in *Royal Valley*.

PLATE 7.

1. The dignified granite frontage to Chapel Court in Justice Street was designed by John Smith (1781-1852), Aberdeen's first City Architect. Formerly known as "Skipper Scott's Close", it was through this pend that King James VIII and III rode on the afternoon of 23rd December, 1715.

2. The armorial bearings of Thomas Menzies of Pitfodels surmounted by the Royal arms of Scotland. Menzies, who acted as Marischal Depute of Scotland in 1538, was appointed Comptroller of the Royal Household in 1543. He died in 1576. A remarkably fine example of heraldic carving, it is built into the wall of a property at the rear of No. 35 Belmont Street.

PLATE 8.

1. One of Elizabeth Blackwell's botanical drawings in *A Curious Herbal* (Vol. I) which she published in 1737. The second volume appeared two years later.

2. The stout, iron-bound doorway of the condemned cell in Aberdeen's old tolbooth.

3. The tolbooth is one of the most interesting buildings in the city. Built in the form of a keep-tower, its narrow spiral staircase gives access to the grim, barrel-vaulted cells.

PLATE 9.

1. The tomb-effigies of Provost Gilbert Menzies of Findon and his wife Marjory de Camera (Chalmers) of Cults. Originally located in the 13th century chapel of the Knights Templars at Maryculter, they were removed *circa* 1890 to the West Church of St. Nicholas, Aberdeen, where they are preserved.

2. General Patrick Gordon of Auchleuchries.

3. Admiral Thomas Gordon.

4. Field Marshal Keith.

5. Prince Barclay de Tollie.

PLATE 10.

1. "Friendville" from the south-east. The gablet, with its semi-circular-headed window, is typical of the 18th century.

2. The tablet built into the north wall of the kirkyard at East St. Clement's Church, commemorating the gift made in 1650 by George Davidson of Pettens. The arms depicted are not those of Davidson of Cairnbrogie—as has been suggested—nor are they listed in *An Ordinary of Scottish Arms*.

PLATE 11.

1. This woodcut of the Rev. John Welch (1570-1622), "sometime minister of the Gospel at Ayr", is from a rare pamphlet published in Glasgow (n.d.). Welch married Elizabeth Knox, third daughter of John Knox, the Reformer, by his second marriage. Their son Nathaniel Welch was a boarder at Aberdeen Grammar School from 1622 to 1626.

2. Portrait by Sir Joshua Reynolds of Jane Maxwell, Duchess of Gordon. "Duchess Jean" was the second daughter of Sir William Maxwell, 3rd Baronet of Monreith, Wigtonshire.

PLATE 12.

1. The dignified entrance gateway to old St. Paul's Episcopal Church at No. 61 Gallowgate, was built in 1721 to designs by Archibald Jaffray. The church is now derelict and the fate of this remarkably fine piece of street architecture is uncertain. The beautiful wrought-iron grille has already gone and the stonework has suffered damage.

2. View of the Cot-town of Balgownie looking westwards along Bridge Terrace, towards the old Black Nook Alehouse, now a private dwelling.

PLATE 13.

1. This photograph of Woolmanhill was taken about a century ago by George Washington Wilson and shows the house at No. 37 (the doorway behind the hand-cart) where Joseph Robertson, the historian, was born on 17th May, 1810. It was here that his father—and subsequently his mother—carried on a small general merchant's business.

2. The "Hammermen's Well" as it is today—restored after having been a casualty of the "black-out" during the Second World War. Of cast iron, it is an excellent example of a private street-well fed by a spring, before the days of piped water supplies. The "essay" keys opened a side panel releasing the hand pump.

PLATE 14.

1. Silver Archery Medal from the Aberdeen Grammar School collection. The photograph shows the obverse side displaying the arms of John Skene of Newtyle, Foveran, and his motto— *"Sors mihi grata cadet"*. The reverse side bears his name and the date 1674.

2 and 3. Portraits belonging to the National Portrait Gallery of Scotland of Robert Gordon of Kynmonowie, later 1st Baronet of Gordonstoun, and Sir Robert Gordon, 3rd Baronet of Gordonstoun—"The Wizard Laird". Both portraits are on loan to Gordonstoun School.

PLATE 15.

1. This interesting photograph was taken about a century ago and shows the Earl Marischal's granary and store-house in relation to the old burgh of Stonehaven.

2. Long a familiar shop-sign in the Green, this gilded tea-pot advertised the premises of John Adams, tea merchant.

PLATE 16.

1. The Chapter House, Balgownie, from Don Street. The arms of George Cruickshank of Berryhill impaled with those of his wife Barbara Hervie can be seen above the larger archway.

2. Our Ladye's Pity Vault (St. Mary's Chapel) erected *ante* 1437 and built entirely of granite during that remarkable period known locally as the "Granite Interregnum".

PLATE 17.

1. The Quaker Meeting House at Kinmuck.

2. The photograph shows the old house of Auchtavan. Now in ruins, it is an excellent example of the early methods of building construction.

PLATE 18.

1. The arms of Patrick Conn, 4th of Auchry, impaled with those of his wife Margaret Cheyne of Esslemont, now built into the farm-house at Castle of Auchry, Monquhitter. They were the parents of Cardinal George Conn.

2. The will of Mary Bannerman—"the Lady Findrassie"—giving detailed instructions concerning her burial. Dated in Quaker style "the twenty-second day of the fifth month (called March) One thousand seven hundred and four years", it is witnessed by four "weighty Friends"—Robert Gordon, Andrew Jaffray of Kingswells, William Taylor and George Forbes of Brux. The fifth signatory, Daniel Hamilton, is presumably her man of business whose flourish at the end of his signature would not be in keeping with Quaker tradition.

PLATE 19.

1. The figure in granite of Priest Gordon at St. Peter's R.C. School, Nelson Street, was Alexander Brodie's first important commission (1860). It brought him to the fore-front of his profession.

2. Cast iron "pig" three feet in height and dated 1732, used as a "head-stone" to mark the grave of one of Thomas Rawlinson's workmen—probably murdered by the Macdonells. Standing in the remote burial ground at Gairlochy, Kilmallie, Inverness-shire, it is a poignant reminder of a dismal failure.

PLATE 20.

1. Font from Forvie kirk, now preserved at the Manse of Slains. Octagonal in form, it is cut from a block of local granite. The two stones forming the base, are not part of the font.

2. William Dyce's well-known picture *Titian's first essay in colour* in the Aberdeen Art Gallery collection. Painted in 1858, the picture illustrates Ridelfi's statement that Titian when a boy gave the earliest indication of his future eminence as a colorist by drawing a madonna which he coloured with the juices of flowers.

PLATE 21.

1. The parish church at Crimond where David Grant's popular psalm-tune was first sung in 1871 by the choir under their precentor William Clubb.

2. Tilliefruskie is one of the best preserved examples of a Ha'-house on Deeside. The photograph shows the courtyard wall and entrance gateway with the mounting-block on the right.

PLATE 22.

George Washington Wilson's dramatic picture of the corrie on Lochnagar—the first photograph ever taken of this famous mountain. The exposure was made in October, 1854, and pack-ponies were required to carry all the photographic equipment necessary to make the picture.

PLATE 23.

The gift of John Keith, 3rd Earl of Kintore, this charming town-house and tolbooth was built between the years 1737 and 1747. The Council Chamber, recently restored, is on the first floor and is reached by the curved fore-stairs. The doorway in the centre, below the stairs, is the entrance to the burgh's tolbooth.

PLATE 24.

This photograph of the Glas-allt Shiel looking across Loch Muick gives an excellent idea of its utter remoteness. The sandy delta and the deep corrie formed by the turbulent Glas-allt are clearly seen.

APPENDIX

No. 1. In old Scots, the word "Mair" is variously spelt—"Maiour", "Mayor", "Maere" and "Meer" being the most usual forms.

No. 2. St. Fittick's Church at Nigg was founded in the 7th century by the French missionary S. Fiacre—the Patron Saint of Paris taxi-drivers. A later church on the original site was dedicated in 1242 by David de Bernham, Bishop of St. Andrews, and this building continued in use under three denominations—Roman Catholic, Episcopalian and Presbyterian—until 1829 when it was abandoned and allowed to become ruinous. Nigg derives its name from Cormac de Nugg (Nigg), a 13th century Celtic nobleman who owned the lands.

No. 3. Benholm's Lodging, popularly known as the Wallace Tower, was unique. Standing just outside the Netherkirkgate Port, it was built on the familiar "Z-plan" for defence and dominated this busy thoroughfare. Its architectural history is given in *Proceedings of the Society of Antiquaries of Scotland* Vol. XCV. Session 1961-62. Edward Meldrum, A.R.I.B.A.,, F.S.A.Scot. A replica of the building, incorporating some of the stones from the original structure, was subsequently built at Tillydrone. This current "Wallace Tower"—in its picturesque but unfortunate setting—is of similar dimensions to the Netherkirkgate building but the claim that it is the original structure "removed stone by stone" to its present site cannot be accepted. The wording on the plaque marking the site of the Wallace Tower in the Netherkirkgate is regrettable. At no time was the building called "Benholm's Lodge" nor was the street in which it stood ever known as the "Nethergate".

No. 4. The story that, while held prisoner at Pitcaple Castle, Montrose was shown a means of escape has recently been clarified—if not confirmed—by the discovery of an underground tunnel leading from the castle to the bank of a nearby stream. This tunnel was linked to the garderobe vent from the room on the second floor where Montrose was confined. A slim person could have crawled without much difficulty down the vent into the tunnel and so made his escape. The lady who showed Montrose this escape route was his cousin Agnes Ramsay of Balmain. She was the wife of John Leslie of Pitcaple who was from home when Montrose was brought prisoner to the castle in May, 1650.

No. 5. Towards the end of last century, a careful search was made
        at St. Giles Cathedral in the crypt where Montrose's remains
        are supposed to have been buried, but no trace of them could
        be found.

No. 6. The Blackwell family lived at *Polmuir*, a delightful residence
        on the lands of Ferryhill overlooking the River Dee. The
        house, which was built by Principal Thomas Blackwell, has
        recently been demolished.

No. 7. The execution of Alexander Blackwell in 1747 is described in
        Scots in Sweden as "the most famous legal murder in
        Swedish history".

No. 8. "Red-beard's Cave", recently obliterated by a landslide,
        was located in the Kincardineshire parish of Durris, on the
        lower eastern slopes of Craigbeg. "Red-beard's Well"—a
        refreshing spring—lies on the east side of the hill-path
        running between Craigbeg and Mongour.

No. 9. In addition to the regimental Gordon tartan designed by
        William Forsyth in 1793, a Huntly tartan—basically red
        and green—was also devised by him. It has been asserted
        that it was made for the exclusive use of the Duke of Gordon
        and his family but this is open to question for the tartan
        appears to have been in general use in the Huntly district
        during the latter part of the 18th century. Two "red"
        Gordon tartans are now in production, the "setts" being
        derived from two historic portraits—(1) Rachel Gordon,
        10th of Abergeldie (1723) and (2) Batoni's well-known
        picture of General the Hon. William Gordon of Fyvie (1766).
        The origin of both these tartans is obscure.

No. 10. A Highland bonnet and other items of dress believed to
        have been worn by the "Duchess Jean" while on her recruit-
        ing campaigns are exhibited in the Gordon Highlanders'
        Museum, St. Luke's, Viewfield Road, Aberdeen.

No. 11. In 1842, a figure of George, 5th and last Duke of Gordon,
        was erected in the Castlegate at Aberdeen. A remarkable
        work in granite by the celebrated sculptor Thomas Campbell,
        it was removed in 1952 and after much controversy, re-sited
        in the centre of Golden Square.

No. 12. The common phrase "gay Gordons" is, of course, a
        misquotation for "gey Gordons". In old Scots, "gey"
        means fast, wild and lawless—rather different from the
        English word "gay".

No. 13. Thomas the Rhymer is said to have been born about the
        year 1220 in the small town of Erceldoun (now called
        Earlston) in Berwickshire.   His name first appears as witness
        to a deed pertaining to Melrose Abbey (1240).   The Rhymer
        would seem to have visited Aberdeen and north-east Scotland
        about the year 1258—then an unknown poet, for thirty
        years were to pass before he achieved fame by predicting
        the tragic death of Alexander III (1249-1286).

No. 14. A posthumous tribute was paid to Joseph Robertson by the
        University of Aberdeen when his portrait was included in
        the memorial window in the Mitchell Hall of Marischal
        College.

No. 15. The Meeting House at Kinmuck was built in 1710 by George
        Wines (Wyness), Inverurie.   It is now the only example
        of an original Quaker Meeting House surviving in Scotland.

P